LifeChanging Bible Study

BY
MATT FRIEDEMAN
AND
LISA FRIEDEMAN AUSLEY

LifeChanging Bible Study

BY
MATT FRIEDEMAN
AND
LISA FRIEDEMAN AUSLEY

francis asbury press

Scripture quotations are from The New International Version

Cover and Designer: Vicki New
Cover Photograph: Plainview/iStockphoto
Copyright © 2009 by Matt Friedeman and Lisa Friedeman Ausley

ISBN 978-0-915143-14-6

All rights reserved. Printed in the United States of America.

No part of this book may be reproduced in any form without written permission from Francis Asbury Press.

For information contact

Francis Asbury Press
P.O. Box 7
Wilmore, KY 40390
859-858-4222
E-mail: francisasb@aol.com
Website: www.francisasburysociety.com

Francis Asbury Press is an imprint of The Francis Asbury Society, Inc.

I want to know one thing, the way to Heaven: how to land safe on that happy shore. God himself has condescended to teach the way; for this very end He came from Heaven. He hath written it down in a book! O give me that book! At any price, give me the book of God! I have it: here is knowledge enough for me. Let me be homo unius libri (a man of one book).

— John Wesley

CONTENTS

Dedication 9

Foreword 11

Chapter 1 – *Unveiling What God Has Revealed* 13

Chapter 2 – *Getting Started* 17

Chapter 3 – *Observation: Initial Steps* 29

Chapter 4 – *Observation: Structural Laws* 43

Chapter 5 – *Interpretation* 59

Chapter 6 – *Correlation* 75

Chapter 7 – *Application* 89

Chapter 8 – *Character Study* 105

Chapter 9 – *Topical Study* 119

Chapter 10 – *Word Study* 133

Chapter 11 – *Teaching What Has Been Learned* 147

Chapter 12 – *Inductive Bible Study: A Quick Summary* 159

DEDICATION

To our mother,
Janis Friedeman,
whose choice to follow Jesus made
an eternal difference in our lives.

FOREWORD

It is indeed a pleasure to introduce Matt Friedeman's and Lisa Friedeman Ausley's creative and practical book, *LifeChanging Bible Study*. It offers new, interesting and effective ways to study the Bible. Not merely an armchair reflection on the matter at hand, *LifeChanging Bible Study* is a book to use. In the best sense of the term, it is a "how to" book.

When Lisa Ausley was a seminary senior, she targeted her senior project on Bible study and its effect on one's Christian life. Lisa's excellent project offered, in nascent form, a number of the concepts that enrich this book. Frankly, I adopted a number of her ideas for my own course on "Teaching the Bible to Youth and Adults." In the intervening years, Lisa has tested her insights about Bible study through teaching and pastoral ministry in local churches. In the meantime, her brother, Matt Friedeman, completed his Ph.D. with a focus in teaching. A truly gifted teacher and communicator, Matt brings his own unique insights to this text. Effective Bible study has equipped Matt for seminary teaching, prison preaching, church planting and pastoring, as well as serving as a newspaper columnist and a daily radio talk show host.

LifeChanging Bible Study has already been refined as a textbook for Bible study at the level of the local church, college, and even seminary. I rejoice to see it offered to a wider public. Again and again, I have seen the effectiveness of this book proven over the years. One enthusiastic student even told me that a seminary course employing an earlier version of *LifeChanging Bible Study* was the most useful in preparing him for his ministry. I believe that this well-designed tool will help many other Christians learn how to study the Word of God.

Harold W. Burgess
2009

CHAPTER 1

Unveiling What God Has Revealed

God is a Revealer.

He has revealed Himself to people, and the story of the revealing and revealed God is written in a book. John Wesley said that he wanted *that* book at *any* price! It contained the message, as Wesley understood it, of the meaning of life and the way to heaven. For centuries, studying the Bible has evoked similar passion and appreciation. Studying that Book, understanding it and delivering the life-changing message contained within its pages, is what Christian communication is all about.

One of the most productive approaches to biblical study is known as *inductive Bible study*. This volume will give readers a brief historical review of the method and demonstrate how to move from the

- study of the text to
- personal application and
- effective communication of the Word.

This approach to Bible study will help modern communicators of truth in one of their most critical challenges. Author and pollster, George Barna, in *Generation Next* notes that three out of four teenagers assert that the Bible provides a reliable characterization of moral truth; *but* a large majority of these same individuals maintain that there is no such thing as absolute truth. Barna believes that one reason for this discrepancy is that, while many teens are willing to say that the Bible is true, they have not studied it for themselves. They are not necessarily opposed to its precepts; the Bible is simply not a part of their lives. Barna's data, as well as that of other researchers, would indicate that what is true of teens is substantially mirrored by other demographic groups, including persons in the ministry. If the concepts of biblical authority and scriptural truth, and their ramifications, are to be counted as relevant to contemporary culture, a serious and responsible study of Scripture must be integrated into the life of every believer and into the education program of the church.

Every chapter of this book is designed to demonstrate how inductive Bible study can broaden the horizons for both teacher and student in today's Christian communities. This volume will explain inductive study in a step-by-step method and then illustrate implementation of that method across a variety of applications: entire books, units within a book, character studies, topical investigations, and key word studies. Finally, we will demonstrate how to use the findings of inductive study to create an effective lesson presentation.

The basic method of induction is known and widely implemented and is not simply used for Bible study. Some would describe it as the scientific method that assumes little to nothing while examining the data at hand and applying intensive investigative methods to determine where the findings might lead.

■ ***Observation*** of the raw material is the first step.

- ■ ***Interpretation*** and a question-answer approach applied to the observations follow.

- ■ ***Correlating*** the passage being studied with other relevant Scripture, life experiences and extra-biblical data is critical.

- ■ ***Application***, or what a scientist might call a *testing of findings*, is where the laboratory of life comes in. All too often this is the most forgotten or ignored step in the study of Scripture.

- ■ And then, the ***teaching*** of the text becomes the apex where truth is imparted to others.

Martin Luther, in his conversations recorded in the volume *Table Talk*, acknowledged that he was less afraid of the bad religion his movement sought to reform than he was the ingratitude of his own people towards the Bible and its precepts. But, he remarked, those who would commit their lives to Bible study would find Scripture a flowing stream where the elephant could swim and, at the same time, a lamb could walk without getting washed away.

CHAPTER 2

Getting Started

John Wesley deemed Bible study a means of grace—not grace itself, but a means through which the grace of God can flow into our lives. And a Methodist of more recent vintage, the late missionary E. Stanley Jones, noted that study of Scripture was an important "means" with which to *begin*. Commencing with the study of God instead of Scripture means starting off with *one's own* conception of God rather than an informed image based on God's specific revelation in the Word. In contrast, beginning with the rich pages of God's Word gives the investigator the means to understand His holy character and the implications of that character for daily life.

Inductive Bible study is, as its name suggests, careful examination of the raw data or fundamental facts of Scripture. Such study over time results in responsible and well-informed conclusions for the diligent Christian. Inductive study emphasizes firsthand observation with an approach that is, as far as is possible, objective. The study method is designed to elicit a thorough examination of the particulars of Scripture from which appropriate insights and conclusions can be drawn.

Bible Study in History

Inductive Bible study has a history as long as the biblical canon itself. However, the deliberate technique that bears the designation "inductive" is a relatively recent phenomenon whose beginnings can be traced to the early and mid-twentieth century. Before we get to that modern development, let's look briefly at Scripture study across the sweep of Western and American history.

The Bible has long been an important addition to school curricula in the United States and in the broader Western civilization as a necessity for understanding the impact of Christianity and the Bible on faith and culture. In religious private schools, memorization of certain doctrinal facts and of the text itself has been the norm. In public schooling, Scripture has at times been utilized as literature and frequently read with the same sense of purpose as any classic.

In modern general education, inductive Bible study, per se, has been little used. In most educational institutions, when the Bible has been studied, it has been employed as part of a curriculum intent on contributing to cultural literacy. With this approach, the desired outcome is to gain a sweeping grasp of the major stories while familiarizing students with historically consequential passages such as the Ten Commandments or the Sermon on the Mount. Modern public education in America, in particular, has been cautious about teaching faith in a pluralistic society with a court system that casts a wary eye towards biblical instruction. Well-informed conclusions based on careful analysis and interpretation of the Bible have not, therefore, been the aim of most general education institutions.

Christian education has by its nature taken a different approach. Studying the Bible to arrive at fundamental religious precepts is the essence of Christian and Jewish education, albeit the traditions differ as to what comprises the canon. Even so, a survey of study techniques across the ages reveals some decidedly flawed methods.

Occasionally, for instance, earlier Jewish scholars sometimes seized upon an overly nuanced mode of observation and interpretation. An example is pointed out in Marvin Wilson's excellent volume *Our Father Abraham*, where it is noted that the letter "l" in *lamed* (teach) was formed in the shape of a goad used for prodding along the one to be trained. This is interesting, but is it exegetically responsible?

Early Christian attempts to illuminate biblical truth sometimes lapsed into less than accurate patterns of interpretation. Justin Martyr (second century) and other Church fathers frequently made substantial leaps of analysis as they attempted to find the person of Jesus in the Old Testament through allegorical interpretation. Clement (third century) claimed such allegories were evident to a "higher" Christian but not the commoner. Augustine (fourth/fifth century) digressed into such fanciful interpretation as, for instance, the door of Noah's ark symbolizing the wound in Jesus' side. It is said of Luther (sixteenth century) that at times he was willing to critique the Bible—and throw out at least three books of the accepted canon—in order that the Word might fit his theology rather than vice versa. So, even these brilliant men of Christian history exhibited occasional flaws in their handling of Scripture. Their sometimes defective approaches could easily lead contemporaries to agree that the Church has struggled with a proper implementation of observation, interpretation, correlation and practice of biblical truth.

So, proponents of inductive Bible study in the modern era saw the need for a standard, easily employed method. Building on centuries of Christian tradition and scholarship, this system of study sought to help students of Scripture apply a common pattern of procedures so that all who desired could examine for themselves biblical truth.

The man who led the modern movement of methodical Bible study was Dr. Wilbert Webster White (1863-1944), known as the "father of inductive Bible study" by his many distinguished students. White's biographer, Charles Eberhardt, wrote that White wanted to help his students become independent, humble, investigators of the truth. White sought to equip his students to provide stimulating biblical insights with nothing more than their Bible and a dictionary.

White founded The Biblical Seminary in New York and insisted that the study of the Bible in the mother tongue of the student should be the central organizing dynamic of the curriculum. He felt that more study should be done in the Bible and less about it, not only during seminary but throughout the life and work of the minister. In fact, White asserted that he founded The Biblical Seminary because of what the seminary had not done for him. He had been trained to consult commentaries and the great thinkers. However, he eventually found greater spiritual and intellectual benefit through inductive Bible study. Using this method, for instance, when studying Ephesians he could listen to Paul himself instead of a well-meaning biographer, commentator or interpreter. As White's excitement about his own firsthand study of the Bible grew, he began sharing his keys to an enlightening experience of the Word. Training independent, competent and original students of the Bible became White's life aim.

Many seminarians learned White's methods and in turn articulated them all over the world. Among the most prominent of those in the shadow of White's long influence is Robert Traina, who later wrote *Methodical Bible Study*. That textbook has become a modern day classic and thoroughly explains the step-by-step method of inductive Bible study. In his volume, Traina compares the proficient Bible student to a good detective. The detective must be skilled in certain procedures, knowing how and where to look for clues. Having gathered the data, the investigator must then correctly interpret it, evaluate it, and draw accurate conclusions based on his findings. Traina called for more Scriptural detectives and, in his long and prominent career first at The Biblical Seminary of New York and then at Asbury Theological Seminary, trained many such biblical investigators.

Since the publication of *Methodical Bible Study*, numerous authors have attempted to simplify and contemporize Traina's insights into workbooks, summaries and seminars. Perhaps the most widespread contemporary movement that seeks to equip laypeople for inductive Bible study is Kay Arthur's *Precept Ministries*, which holds training sessions worldwide to encourage and teach the principles and methodology of inductive Bible study.

Important Preliminaries

The first step to Bible study should always be the same: prayer. A prayerful approach assumes that study of the Bible is not merely familiarization with a great literary classic. It is the study of the inspired Word, God's revelation to mankind. At issue here is the study of a "living" text, one that truly has power through God's Spirit to transform and inspire.

As we approach the Word of God, we should humbly and prayerfully invite His presence. A prayerful attitude prepares the student's heart to receive Life from the pages of the text, with the Spirit as tutor and guide. Prayer recognizes that God is a partner in this endeavor and that He wants to add significantly to the process. Dialogue with the Divine convinces us that the glory of discovering Scriptural truth is nothing in which we should boast or gloat. Rather, it is a satisfaction and joy that God Himself can and will succeed in communicating to us in this hour and this day.

The difference between Bible study as tedious, painstaking, exhausting labor *versus* the fulfilling, exhilarating experiences which inspire us to a more obedient life is often one thing: prayer. The first ingredient in a successful approach to Scripture is always a relationship with God!

Take the Wide Angle View First

Upon opening the Book, it is paramount to first get the big picture. By all means, avoid the temptation to begin study by focusing on a favorite verse or passage. One must first study the whole before clearly understanding the parts.

It is nearly impossible to put together a jigsaw puzzle without any vision of the finished image. First, careful observation of the picture on top of the box is helpful. Then, corner and edge pieces are found and fitted into place. These provide a framework or "frame of reference" to which all other pieces relate. Next, major images or themes are put in place before, finally, the less obvious pieces can be added. Starting biblical study with an isolated verse or passage is like picking up random pieces of that puzzle and trying desperately to make them fit.

It is best to begin study with an initial reading of one entire book of the Bible in a single sitting. With an epistle like Ephesians, this is quite manageable. For this reason, it is good advice for a beginning Bible student to start with a shorter book. Tackling a larger portion, like Isaiah, will require more diligence but can be accomplished. Oftentimes, this initial overview of the entire book (e.g., Luke or Genesis) is more skimming than detailed reading, a looking for corners to provide a frame of reference for the study which will follow.

Because the Bible was written one book at a time, each one has its own unique message within God's total revelation. Each has its particular author, its own unique audience, and therefore its specific purpose. Each book within the Bible has its historical context, its flavor and style, its themes and the structure which holds chapters and verses together. Isolated verses can be confusing and meaningless unless considered in context of the whole. Therefore, begin by getting the "bird's eye view" and then proceed to the "worm's eye view."

Initially Avoid the Work of Others

The very definition of induction demands that the vernacular text itself be the primary basis for study (although external helps such as lexicons, grammars, dictionaries, concordances, and historical background can be useful in firsthand study). The student examining the text strives to approach God's Word with a clean slate—with no preconceived notions about its meaning. This is difficult enough to do given one's already developed opinions and notions about matters of faith and issues of theology. Initial use of a pile of commentaries and other books about the Bible only exacerbates the problem.

Consulting the findings of writers and theologians should be a final step after one's own thoughtful and careful study has been completed. Relying on the interpretations of others may be enlightening, but it destroys the very purpose of the inductive approach and should be "shelved" until firsthand observation and interpretation are completed.

God's truth can be compared to the shining stars in the night sky. They are beautiful from a penthouse suite located in a huge metropolis with thousands of city lights glowing all around. But that view cannot compare with the brilliance of those celestials viewed from a hillside on deserted Wyoming acreage on a cloudless night. Each constellation stands out in clarity, its luminescence breathtaking. In those environs the observer can seemingly see forever. So it is with God's Word. Focusing on the Scripture alone with no other "lights" shining enables fresher and more personal discoveries of God's truth.

Even so, we will concede that after those discoveries are made, surveying the conclusions of others can be helpful. We concur with Charles Spurgeon who noted that the student of Scripture should avoid opposing pitfalls: taking everything secondhand from others, and at the opposite end of the continuum, refusing to glean anything from others.

Which Translation?

In inductive Bible study, the type of tool employed significantly determines the outcome of the work. Just as the surgeon requires precise instruments, the one who dissects the Word also needs precision. This is why all inductive study must be done with a translation, rather than with a paraphrased version of the Bible.

Paraphrased versions such as the popular initial editions of *The Living Bible* or *The Message* are wonderful additions to a resource library, but are not adequate for inductive study as they are not exact translations from the original languages, Hebrew and Greek. Also, it is a good practice to stick to a single translation, provided it is an excellent one. This provides consistency as one works through the Bible and aids as well in memorization.

Which translation is best? Obviously, there are many differences of opinion, but the *New International Version (NIV)* is our pick. As Gordon D. Fee and Douglas Stuart suggest in *How to Read the Bible for All Its Worth*, the NIV was translated by a committee representing the best scholarship in the evangelical tradition. The *NIV* is also a beneficial choice given its widespread use. To communicate insights in the version most people hold in their hands is a definite advantage. For this reason, Christian educators in mainline Protestant denominations might consider the *New Revised Standard Version,* when appropriate, and Catholics, for instance, might prefer the *New American Bible*.

Further, for inductive Bible study, use a Bible without notes or study guides, as viewing the scholarly insights of study Bibles is simply observing the work of others before completing one's own unbiased study.

Approach the Discipline with Discipline

The most significant ingredient in the art of Bible study is diligence. Nothing can replace personal discipline. Learning and pursuing a systematic, methodical study of the Bible is a lifelong process and, frankly, a demanding one. But it is a rewarding means of learning, and neglecting it is clearly unacceptable for the earnest Christian.

There is no shortcut to the mastery of inductive Bible study just as there is no shortcut to maturity. Growth does not always occur overnight, but the disciplined mental and spiritual training that results in a serious approach to Scripture will bear increasing fruit.

Although many people never get beyond a simple reading and rereading of Scripture, the mechanics of inductive Bible study and the discipline that necessarily accompanies it is vital to a dedicated Christian life. Even though many of the steps of inductive study might initially seem laborious, as Traina states in *Methodical Bible Study*, one shouldn't confuse tediousness with insignificance. Just as a musician meticulously practices finger exercises, scales, timing and form, the Bible student should gladly discipline himself in the mastery of the mechanics of Bible study.

However, it likewise follows that one's study of Scriptures never reaches completion, just as one never achieves complete maturity in every area of life. For one thing, our own personal growth enables us to see more clearly the truths of Scripture today than was possible yesterday. Secondly, the very nature of Scripture makes its study inexhaustible. No matter how much we partake of the Text, the supply doesn't diminish. No study, regardless of how comprehensive, will capture the total truth of Scripture or exhaust the countless possible insights.

A Means, Not an End

The last principle essential to successfully navigating the journey to effective Bible study is this: inductive Bible study is simply a means to the end. It is not, as mentioned earlier, the end in itself. Kay Arthur states in her text, *How to Study Your Bible*, that study of Scripture has as its goal to draw us into our own personal interaction with Scripture and therefore with the God of Scripture. In doing so, it shapes our beliefs, which are based on prayerful understanding and legitimate interpretation of God's Word. That truth, then, transforms us when we live by it.

So the real danger in the inductive, careful, meticulous study of Scripture is that one might get lost in the mechanics of it. It is possible to forget that the method is intended to train our minds to understand the message of Scripture, to see clearly so that truth is not overlooked, to slow down and listen obediently so that God's Spirit can speak the mysteries of His Word to our minds, and to practice the truth that has been recognized.

The means, then, is our careful study of Scripture. The end is our living by it and allowing God to transform us—our relationship with Him, our character, our thoughts, our attitudes, our actions and indeed, our entire approach to life. And this transformation comes, again, through the truth of Scripture, which leads us to better know and love the Author of Scripture. It is in knowing and loving Him that we are truly transformed.

In summary then, inductive Bible study incorporates six principles fundamental to mastering the heart and purpose of the method:

- The first step is always conversation with God.
- The investigator starts with the big picture.
- The biblical text comes first, then other "helps."
- The text utilized should be a translation, not a paraphrase.

GETTING STARTED

> - Diligence is essential.
>
> - Inductive study is not the end, but the means to an end.

The late Princeton professor Emile Cailliet, in his autobiography titled *Journey Into Light*, recalls a leather-bound pocket book he had filled with passages from favorite books. He dubbed his self-made volume *The Book That Understands Me*. In what seemed divine timing, his wife came home one day with a Bible at the exact moment that Cailliet had opened up and was perusing his volume under a tree. The young Cailliet was finding, much to his disappointment, that the various passages he had recorded were less than satisfying because, alas, they were of his own choosing. He grabbed the Bible from his wife—though he had heretofore forbidden her to have one because of its religious content—and rushed to his study. Opening it, he read and read and read and the discovery rushed in upon him: It was *this* Book that understood him more than anything he could have compiled himself. Cailliet's study eventually propelled him into a lifetime of teaching ministry.

CHAPTER 3

Observation: Initial Steps

John Calvin, reformer and one of the greatest intellects of Christian history, said that the person who really studied Scripture would find it immutable and eternal. To suppose that Scripture is only transient and temporary was tragic. In fact, he thought such a supposition was virtually diabolical. Thus, it was incumbent on believers to diligently *read* and *attend* to the Bible. Reading, of course, begins the process of acquaintance with the Book of books. But the word *attending* is a bit different. It intimates something more, requiring additional effort. Thus, inductive study starts with reading, but it also takes seriously this *attending to*, or as we make the case here, *observing carefully what we read*.

"Observation is the act of seeing things," said late Princeton Seminary professor, H.T. Kuist, "as they really are." It is the first step (following prayer) in inductive Bible study and the key to all that follows. For without careful and methodical discovery, the necessary and subsequent steps of interpretation, correlation and application rest on the subjective grounds of individual analysis and prejudiced examination.

On the following pages of this chapter, the reader will learn what to look for in a portion of Scripture in order to proceed with a careful observation of the passage under inquiry. These recommendations, coupled with the suggestions in the next chapter, will give the careful reader of Scripture a solid foundation from which to proceed to proper interpretation, correlation and application of the verses studied. Indeed, the learner will likely find with these few simple steps that the Bible will begin revealing more than he ever imagined it could. That is the joy of the inductive method—you investigate what has been on the printed page for centuries but with some simple steps of observation it offers a freshness that is engaging.

This act of observation is to Bible study what the foundation is to a building. The substructure of a building must be carefully laid and must provide a solid base for the planned edifice. Care is taken at this initial step of the building, though no longer visible when construction is complete, it holds all the rest firmly in place. So it is with observation in Bible study. Careful work at this stage might not be apparent to those who later receive the lesson derived from the study, but it allows interpretation and application to be properly and engagingly implemented.

In modern education circles, this step might be understood as the initial phase of what has become well-known as discovery learning. Discovery learning is a process whereby teachers and learners directly investigate a subject rather than relying on what others think, have said or have published. The best way to facilitate such learning, of course, is to let the student proceed in his own determination of the basic facts. Something learned firsthand can never be adequately replaced by intellectual spoon feedings, or information verbally transferred from the "expert" to "the ignorant."

Jon Amos Comenius (1592-1670) is probably the most noteworthy among many educators through the last several centuries to accentuate the need to *learn by actually doing.* He proposed that the collection of data and the organizing, comparing and contrasting of those facts comprised the best foundation for learning. In fairness, much of what Comenius did was to turn his students to the sensory perception of the natural world. But recognizing the importance of the spiritual world, he also took seriously the firsthand exploration of instruction of the written word and believed that one should arrive at conclusions through firsthand investigation.

Etienne Bonnet de Condillac (1715-1780) was educated as a priest but known for his work as a French philosopher. He subscribed to this same approach of sense impression or firsthand experience. While he dealt with topics beyond the written word, his five steps describing the acquisition of knowledge through sensation correlate closely with the observation phase of inductive Bible study as described in our next two chapters:

- Observing primary matter (for our purposes, the Bible)

- Noting the relationships within the primary matter, objects or phenomenon

- Observing the space, or intervals, between the matter or objects

- Observing the secondary objects/matter/phenomenon that fill the space/intervals

- Comparing/contrasting all that has been observed

After these steps, de Condillac suggested that interpretation of this data should occur and an unbiased principle be derived.

In recent decades, Hilda Taba and her work in the Contra Costa School District in California led the way for many in modern public educational circles to consider inductive processes in the classroom. Her ideas have relevance at each point of the main suggestions of this book and, because of her profound research and thinking on the method at large, will be referred to at each fundamental step of the process. Taba maintained that the first step in the inductive thinking model was concept formation. Concept formation is the result of elicited questions; the study and listing of data; a grouping of common and contrasting properties regarding the subject of investigation; and then labeling, categorizing and developing a hierarchical order of super- and sub-ordination. This accomplished, interpretation of the data can commence.

For Taba, this first stage of a three-step process worked superbly in her own setting of an elementary school social studies program. Since the inductive method is neither age- nor subject-bound, the inductive process is compatible with a range of subjects and educational stages. What is true for a variety of academic subjects is undoubtedly true for Bible study as well. With this premise we begin digging deeper into the concept of observation as the primary key to inductive study of the Word of God.

Before reviewing helpful hints for observing a passage of Scripture, some basic steps should be noted.

First, the inductive Bible study method always works best when the passage being studied is examined as if it were the first time one has ever seen it. A wise professor once said that the end of all education is ignorance—a questioning mind! That is a good observational principle.

Second, take notes on a piece of paper, in your Bible or with a notepad. Our own conviction here is simple—the Bible of one engaged in inductive study should be a well-marked friend.

Third, try to see how many different observations you

can make concerning a passage. The more time spent on this step, the more fruitful avenues of interpretation, correlation and application become possible. *The Student, the Fish, and Agassiz* is an essay that first appeared in a periodical of the late nineteenth century. It has emerged many times since, not the least for use in explaining the observational principles of the inductive method. As the story goes, the professor, Agassiz, slaps a fish in front of the student and asks him to describe what he sees. Ten minutes later, the student has exhausted the possibilities. But since the professor has left the student alone for a considerable time, the student begins to draw the fish and with closer observation sees details he had never noticed before. The professor appears pleased but wants more. The student is frustrated, goes home, comes back another day and, still challenged by the professor, suddenly blurts out that the professor must want to know that the fish has symmetrical sides and paired organs. The professor leaves again, allowing the student to develop a new catalog of findings. Now seeing his subject in a little different focus, he continues. Eventually, another fish is laid before the student and comparisons and contrasts are made. And eventually, eight months later, the student moves on to insects.

The point is this: Once you think you know all there is to know about a subject, you may well know only some of what other people know about a subject. Lasting education comes from firsthand and thorough examination. And the observation that has been completed is never really complete.

Fourth, select units instead of just a few sentences for study. Some of the best observation comes from studying a book-as-a-whole. Once that is accomplished, studying sections-as-a-whole, chapters-as-a-whole and paragraphs-as-a-whole is profitable as well. Getting the big picture first provides vital insight.

Fifth, in order to observe thoroughly it is necessary to read the unit under observation several times. This approach is obviously more feasible with smaller units but it no less helpful with larger sections of text.

As we travel through this volume together, the authors challenge you to select a unit of study and proceed through these steps in the true inductive spirit—hands-on practice. One place to start is with a moderately-sized epistle like Ephesians. For consistency, throughout this volume we will illustrate inductive Bible study principles with reference to that book, as well as other selected portions of Scripture. We recommend that you either follow along the ensuing pages with Ephesians wide open or emulate the steps with a book of your own choice.

Ask the Obvious Questions

Journalism students are taught from the start of their training the frontline questions of good reporting: *Who, What, When, Where, How* and *Why*. When applied to the Bible, they produce many avenues of insight and of further investigation. Indeed, the more painstakingly these questions are asked of Scripture, the more they tend to reveal.

- Who are the major characters?

- What is written? What is said? What are the major ideas and teaching?

- When is it written? When is it said? When did the event take place? When will the event take place?

- Where in the book is it written or said? From where is it being written? To where is it being written? Where is it going to happen?

- How is it written or said? How did the event take place?

- Why is this event happening? Why is this person saying this? Why is it necessary? Why is this story told? Why is this teaching included? Why does this unit come before or after that unit? Why does the teaching or writing matter to those involved?

Let's try applying these questions to the first chapter of Ephesians and just the first three verses. Our answers won't be exhaustive, but will illustrate one of the initial steps of observation.

Pericope: Ephesians 1:1-3

¹Paul, an apostle of Christ Jesus by the will of God,
To the saints in Ephesus, the faithful in Christ Jesus:
²Grace and peace to you from God our Father and the Lord Jesus Christ. ³Praise be to the God and Father of our Lord Jesus Christ, who has blessed us in the heavenly realms
with every spiritual blessing in Christ.

Who: Paul, saints in Ephesus, Christ Jesus, God, God our Father

What: Offerings of grace and peace and a command to praise

When: Has blessed us—past tense

Where: Ephesus

Why: (Inference) Because the Ephesians are saints and faithful

How: By the will of God; in Christ

These observations have been made on a relatively few verses of Scripture and without the benefit of reading the book as a whole. If the same observations were made on the entire epistle, the lists of answers would run for pages. Compiling pages of data might be the aim of a budding scholar of Ephesians; but given time, interest and purpose, a more general listing would also be profitable. To demonstrate, let's answer the questions for the book-as-a-whole with brief but important answers.

Pericope: *Ephesians*

Who: Paul, Ephesians, God (Father, Son, Spirit) are the main characters.

What: This epistle is a message from Paul to the Ephesians to broaden their perspective of abundant living. The first half is about the cosmic calling of Paul and the Ephesians; the second half is about the effects that issue from that cosmic call.

When: The letter apparently arrives when the Ephesians need to hear the expanding and encouraging message Paul has for them.

Where: Ephesus is the place where the saints are.

Why: The first three chapters, which are doctrinal in nature, provide the "why" of the last three, which are practical. The Ephesians have been the recipients of an amazing array of spiritual blessings (and need to know it): they have been made alive in Christ, they have been made one with the chosen nation of Israel, they have been blessed by God's ministry to them through Paul. Now, since they are aware of these things, they need to conduct their lives worthy of this high calling.

How: The Ephesians are to respond to God's grace and generosity towards them and to live out that response in

> very practical ways: seeking unity in the Body of Christ, paying close attention to the details of lifestyle choices, love/submission/obedience, and understanding the realities of spiritual warfare.

A more general rendering of questions-answers to Ephesians ought to give the reader a good summary of what the book is all about. To a certain extent, it is possible to get virtually the same information from the introduction in a good study Bible. But *commentary-free observation* is vital to the inductive learning process. It impacts the intellect far more than merely reading someone else's synopsis of the text.

John Locke, in his *Essay Concerning Human Understanding*, probably said it most plainly. He suggested that until learners see things with their own eyes and perceive with their own understanding, real learning will be stunted. Seeing through another person's eyes darkens the view.

Look for Key Words or Phrases

Frequently key words and phrases are repeated numerous times. In Leviticus, for instance, a key word is "holy" as evidenced by its recurrent use. In Matthew "kingdom" is common. In Ephesians, the following words or phrases occur frequently:

- church
- power
- glory(ious)
- love/d
- Spirit
- grace
- power

A couple of words are uniquely repetitious:

- "Mystery" appears seven times in Ephesians, but only 25 times in the entire Bible.
- "Riches" is seen but five times in the same book, but this is significant since there are only 17 mentions in the whole New Testament.

Look for both kinds of *key words*—those that *occur frequently* and those that are *relatively unique* to the epistle or book. The more the learner does Bible study, the more apt one is to be able to pick out the latter.

Examine for Other Major Clues

Look for any clues to:
- purpose
- literary form
- comparisons
- contrasts
- questions
- connectives
- grammar and
- tone

A quick review of each category follows:

a. Purpose: Why did the author write this? What did the author hope to accomplish? What did characters involved in the writing desire to accomplish with their words or actions? Why did God want Christians thousands of years later to read it?

In Ephesians, the "why" must be inferred from the data. It would seem that Paul sensed a need for the churched to grasp their standing with God and its implications. It has the sense of a pep talk, or of a divine broadening of their perspective in God.

b. Literary form: Which form best identifies the unit

you are studying? Is it historical, biographical, poetic, proverbial, prophetic, an epistle/letter or some combination? Genesis is an example of history with a recurring biographical element. Psalms and Proverbs would constitute poetic and proverbial forms, respectively. The last twelve books of the Old Testament are purely prophetic. Paul's epistles are letters, of which Ephesians is one.

Other minor literary forms include discourse, narrative, parabolic and apocalyptic materials.

c. Comparison: Look for the *connection of similar things*. In Matthew, for instance, Jesus frequently points out that "the Kingdom of heaven is like . . ." In Ephesians, the armor of God section of chapter six contains interesting, picturesque comparisons of what truth, righteousness, the gospel of peace, faith and salvation ought to constitute in the life of the believer.

d. Contrast: Contrast is the *connection of dissimilar things*. Psalm 1 provides a striking example of contrast, with the righteous and wicked placed side by side. Sometimes contrast can be a major theme in a book. For instance, in the gospels Jesus' ministry is often contrasted with that of the scribes and Pharisees. Chapter two of Ephesians contrasts a once dead spiritual state with the current vitality of the saints.

e. Questions: The use of interrogation is always of interest. Sometimes the question is rhetorical, sometimes it is used to dissect an argument and sometimes it is a clear inquiry. Note where, when and why the question mark appears. In the gospels Jesus uses questions for a number of reasons. Paul employs them liberally in Romans to make important points, challenge thinking and also add a dialogical tone. In Ephesians, he makes a Christological point using the question mark—look for it in chapter four.

f. Connectives: These are words that reveal relationships within units.

- "But," "yet," "nevertheless," "however" and "instead" introduce contrast (Ephesians 4:20).
- "As," "just as," "like" and "likewise" lead to comparisons (Ephesians 2:1; 4:1; 4:32; 5:2).
- "If" is an important conditional word.
- "In order that" and "so that" indicate purpose (Ephesians 2:7).
- "For," "for this reason," "because," "therefore" and "then" indicate reason and results (Ephesians 1:15; 3:14; 4:25).
- Look for temporal connectives: "After," "as," "before," "now," "then," "until," "when" and "while" (Ephesians 3:10; 5:8, 6:13).
- "First of all," "last of all," "finally" and "or" will lead to a series of facts (Ephesians 6:10).

g. Grammar: Verbs, nouns, pronouns, adverbs and adjectives are always worth noting when observing a unit of study. Are the verbs, for instance, in the famous "armor of God" passage in Ephesians (6:13-18) critical to understanding these sentences?

h. Tone: Is the tone joyous? Angry? Concerned? What is the mood of Galatians? Compare that epistle with I Thessalonians. Why is the tenor of the letter varied? The tone in Ephesians seems to be encouraging, instructive and challenging.

Look for Commands, Promises, Positive/Negatives

Commands in most books of the Bible, including Pauline material, are usually easy to spot. In the fifth and sixth chapters of Ephesians, Paul issues commands to all members of the nuclear family. Ephesians doesn't appear to contain any promises, but an encouraging exercise in Scripture is to keep an eye out for the promises of God. It can also be a bit chilling when God promises punishment if people don't live up to the precepts before them. Compiling characteristics, both positive and negative, of important biblical personalities is usually an enlightening exercise, and Ephesians is no exception. An intriguing list could easily be assembled on God in His various Persons, or on Paul, or on the Ephesians themselves.

Make a Chart

If Ephesians as a whole were depicted in graphic form, each chapter could carry a three to five word title briefly describing the contents therein. But in the study of any passage of Scripture one should remember that chapter breaks are someone else's editorial decision, and in our estimation, not always good decisions. Since inductive Bible study should approach the unit without any preconceived notions, it is wise to try to initially ignore the placement of chapter titles and paragraph breaks in the text and decide for oneself where the divisions should occur.

It would be profitable to *name the chapters and represent these brief resumés on a chart*. The bottom part of the chart should indicate sections as the reader determines them. Here is an example of Ephesians' chapter titles and section breakdowns.

Living the Calling

1	2	3	4	5	6
Blessings in Christ	Alive and One!	The Preacher and a Prayer	A Worthy Life	Imitators of God: Husbands and Wives	Children, Slaves and The Armor of God

Blessing of the Calling (cause)			A Living Worth the Calling (effect)					
Greeting (1:1-2)	The Divine Purpose (1:3-14) / The Prayer of Paul (1:15-23)	Progress Towards God's Purpose (2:1-3:21)	Unity in Christ (4:1-16)	Putting On New Self (4:17-32)	Becoming Imitators of God (5:1-21)	Personal Relationships (5:22-6:9)	Cosmic Battle (6:10-20)	Salutation (6:21-24)

Chapter titling provides a helpful exercise in surveying and briefly synopsizing the text. But, again, chapter breaks are not usually the best way to order a book for a thorough understanding of the unit, which is why section breaks of the student's devising are preferable.

What makes a chart like this so helpful is that it is memorable, and can be helpful for quick and easy reference at a later date. Further additions to such a chart that will add even more clarity to the structure of a book will be demonstrated in the next chapter in our review of Genesis.

When the unit being studied is less than the book-as-a-whole (cf. the subsections as seen in the foregoing chart), it is helpful to make paragraph titles. They can be created in the same way as chapter titles when studying at the "big picture" level as seen above in Ephesians (the book as a whole).

Section breaks obviously should be more specific than in the book-as-a-whole study. One of the major reasons is that excellent unit studies can be drawn from the sections noticed in the book-as-a-whole. For Ephesians, either the first three or final three chapters could be studied as separate units. If we were interested in a more complete investigation of church unity as described in Ephesians, we could study in depth the three or four paragraphs that address that topic in the fourth chapter.

The kind of observation discussed in this chapter is excellent preparation for the next chapter, where we will explore the interesting relationships within the book and questions that lead to an even deeper knowledge of what the God of the Bible is trying to relate to us. Observation in inductive Bible study is frequently accompanied by the words "I never saw that before." The beauty of Bible study in the inductive tradition is that no matter how practiced the student—whether beginner or seasoned scholar—there is always new insight to be discovered.

CHAPTER 4

Observation: Structural Laws

Suppose you were the coach of a soccer team, and at the end of the year your spouse wanted to recount the story of your season in the annual Christmas letter. The account could be written in a number of ways:

- How your last season was so bad, and this one so good, that you could only *compare* it to the unlikely losing, and then winning, seasons of the World Series champions '69 New York Mets (the law of comparison)

- How poorly your son, the star player, performed at the beginning of the season *contrasted* with how good he was the last four games (the law of contrast)

- How that one power play worked every single time you *repeated* it (the law of repetition/recurrence)

- How your team turned the corner at that *crucial* practice and you never lost thereafter (the law of cruciality, or pivot)

- How great coaching *caused* the team to excel (the law of causation)

- A simple blow-by-blow description of every game with the final *summary* of all the season totals (the law of summary)

- The *climactic* last game when everything came together—all the work, all the coaching, all the improvement and a little luck—and you won the championship (the law of climax)

Whether you knew it or not, if any of these approaches were utilized in writing a letter, one or more structural laws were employed. And what would be true of your spouse's missive can also apply to the biblical author of the book you are about to study. Sometimes consciously, sometimes unconsciously, the structural laws are used to make the Christmas letter, the historical account, a piece of poetry or an epistle memorable.

One of the most profitable instruments in the toolbox of the student of Scripture is the awareness of structural laws. These laws help the reader to understand how an author arranged the material in order to obtain maximum impact. Recognizing these laws is one of the most instructive components of inductive Bible study as it facilitates the discovery of the writer's intended effect.

Our study of the structural laws of composition will briefly detail why these laws are effective when studying Scripture and how each can be identified. Upon completion of this chapter, readers will be able to begin to enjoy the great benefits of applying the structural laws first to whole books and then to segments and paragraphs, and the Bible will open up with an abundance of fresh insights.

The initial edition of these laws was first discussed by

John Ruskin in the *Elements of Drawing* (1857), devised for young students to use in their study of nature. He had in mind observation of natural facts, not the study of Scripture.

In the twentieth century, White, Traina and others revised Ruskin's discovery to be used not in the study of nature but in an inquisitive approach to Scripture. The laws in their revised form include the following: **comparison, contrast, repetition, climax, continuation, cruciality, interchange, particularization/generalization, causation, analysis, interrogation, preparation/introduction, summarization and harmony.**

Identifying these structural laws in a given passage is best accomplished after a thorough reading (actually, several readings) of the book, section, paragraph or sentence being examined. When the first wave of observational questions and answers (as described in chapter three) have been made, the structural laws should then be considered.

> Caution: As with anything new, the initial application of these laws by the budding practitioner of inductive Bible study will seem perhaps onerous. With practice, however, they will become easy to identify and extremely useful to the study method. Indeed, vistas of understanding are ahead for the Bible student who seeks mastery of these organizing principles.

Take a Step Back

The use of structural laws is all about seeing relationships between divisions, segments, paragraphs, and sentences within books. It is that *"big picture"* mentioned earlier—examining and understanding how the passage being explored relates within itself to comprise a unit of inspired literature.

Therefore, at whatever level the study is being conducted, whether book divisions, sections within divisions or paragraphs within sections, the application or recognition of structural laws within that unit requires a big-picture perspective. It is a different exercise than picking apart a portion of Scripture with *who, what, when, where, why* and *how* questions. Nor is it the keen eye turned toward grammatical connectives. This is an activity that gets above the data and above the nuances of grammar and the richness of reportorial inquiry, looking broadly across the words, paragraphs, and pages. It is, simply, finding out how the unit being explored fits together, and this can only be accomplished from a self-imposed distancing of sorts.

Test All the Structural Laws

When investigating a unit, determine which laws fit the portion of Scripture you are studying. Occasionally, several laws can be found in a book study. The key is not to identify each law present necessarily, but to *find the major ones* that will lend greater understanding to the intent and literary technique of the author.

Before proceeding any further, let's consider the laws to which we have been referring and a brief description of each. Since "Ephesians" is the book that we are highlighting in our study, whenever a structural law is found in a substantial way in that book, we will note it.

Repetition: **The law of repetition connotes repeated use of a word, phrase or idea.** Most biblical books contain several elements that are relatively unique to that book. In Leviticus, the word "holy" is used many times and thus constitutes one of the key elements of this third book of the Law. In Judges, the Israelites' cycles of disobedience recur throughout the narrative.

When words or phrases are repeated, some students of Scripture find it beneficial to mark their text with a variety of colored pencils. In Ephesians, for instance, the word "mystery" might be marked in red, the words "heavenly realms" in blue, the word "Christ" in gold and the words "love/d" in green. Color-coding obviously makes for easy reference and quick recall.

Additional structural laws, when discovered, should be noted in the margins of the text. Pencil is helpful at this point because, in reference to structural laws, students will occasionally change their minds and want to erase their earlier impression. But a Bible that becomes a holy notepad for observations, particularly with structural laws, is a rich resource for future reference.

Preparation/Introduction: **This law signifies that the reader is being prepared for what follows through background information or the setting of events/ideas.** For example, the first two chapters of the book of Joshua set up the conquest of Canaan in the balance of the book. In Acts, preparation for the coming material is seen in Jesus' challenge and promise to the apostles in that account's first eight verses. They are to be his messengers to the city of Jerusalem, the surrounding geographical regions and the world. That charge constitutes the outline for the rest of the Acts account. Check out Ephesians 1:1-14 for preparatory material in that epistle.

Comparison: **The law of comparison is the comparing of similar things to demonstrate likeness.** The kingdom parables of Matthew 13:24-52 are good examples of comparison. The kingdom of the Lord, in these verses, is like . . . a man . . . a mustard seed . . . yeast . . . treasure . . . a net. Hosea compares the relationship between God and Israel with the prophet's failed marriage. Look for the association of both characters and ideas in Scripture. Ephesians 5:2 compares the life the Ephesians are called to lead to the love and sacrifice of Christ. *Frequent clues: "is like . . . ," "as," "likewise," "so also."*

Contrast: **The law of contrast is also a comparison—of dissimilar things—in order to highlight differences.** Psalm 1, for instance, contrasts the righteous and the wicked. In

Ephesians 2, the former state of spiritual deadness is contrasted with the current state of vitality in the saints at Ephesus. As with comparison, both characters and ideas are contrasted in the Bible. *Frequent clues: the words "but/yet" and "nevertheless."*

Climax: The law of climax follows a gradual progression to the high point of a unit. This law is dramatically demonstrated in the final verses of Exodus when former slaves, prepared throughout the book for a momentous event, witness the glory of the Lord filling the tabernacle. In Matthew a climax occurs in the resurrection of Jesus and the commissioning of the disciples.

Continuation: The law of continuation signifies the extended treatment of a subject and the carrying through to completion of an idea or series of events. It involves extension, rather than merely recurrence. John 1:1-17 is an example of this in a short passage. The "Word" is revealed bit by bit and finally, we are told that it is grace and truth realized in Jesus Christ.

Cruciality/Pivot: The law of cruciality or pivot is seen during narrative units when a definite turn of events takes place. In Numbers 13-14, when the people refuse to possess the promised land, they wander in the wilderness for forty years instead. In Acts 8-9, the scattering of the persecuted believers and the conversion of Saul take the church in an entirely different direction.

Interchange: The law of interchange, a subsidiary law, utilizes alternating elements which frequently strengthen contrasts and comparisons. Luke 1-2 alternates between the John the Baptist and Jesus narratives. I Samuel 1-4 alternates between Hannah and her son Samuel, and Eli and his sons.

**_Particularization/Generalization:_ The law of particularization is the movement from a general statement

to particular ones. One example is Matthew 5:17-48 where Jesus, in the Sermon on the Mount, describes a righteousness surpassing that of the religious authorities of the day and then, in the rest of that unit, details that righteousness in terms of murder, adultery, divorce, oaths, personal disarmament and love for enemies.

The law of generalization is the movement from the particular statements to the general. This principle is seen clearly in James 2:1-13 where the general statement is found in the final sentence of that section: mercy wins over judgment. The foregoing paragraphs particularize that generalization.

Cause and Effect: **The law of causation is the presentation of a cause and a notable result.** Frequently cause is presented first, then result; sometimes the result is presented first, then the cause. The Holy Spirit's advent in chapter two and subsequent events in the book of Acts are a remarkable display of cause-effect. Ephesians chapters 1-3 is a good example of cause; chapters 4-6, the effect. Romans 8:18-30 demonstrates effect-cause, with 28-30 constituting the cause and the preceding verses, the effect. *Frequent clues: "for," "because," "therefore," "then," "since."*

Analysis: **The law of analysis is an event or idea followed by its interpretation.** The sixth chapter of John is a notable example; the Lord multiplies the fish and bread and then proceeds to suggest that He, Jesus, is the Bread of life.

Interrogation: **The law of interrogation is the setting forth of a question or problem and its answer.** The book of Habakkuk is structured significantly around the question/answer dynamic. *Frequent clue—a question mark.* The law of interrogation is not always question and answer, however. Look for problems with solutions like the Noah narrative of Genesis 6-10.

Harmony: **The law of harmony is, as Traina says, not so much a law of composition as a law of truth.** Even so, since harmony is seen through structure the two are virtually inseparable. Harmony is present in promise-fulfillment and in something like disease-remedy. Note the agreement seen in Romans 1:18-3:20 and Romans 3:21ff.

One can see by even a cursory reading of these structural laws that they are interrelated. The disease-remedy of harmony sounds an awful lot like interrogation with its problem-solution; particularization and summary can look similar as well; analysis and continuation are sometimes disputed. Even practiced scholars come up with different answers for the same passage. The important thing is that the identification of one or more of the foregoing laws leads to further questions and responsible answers to critical inquiries.

This list is not all-inclusive. At times an incredibly significant insight from the text can be difficult to categorize. That does not diminish its importance. These laws are a guide, not a sure destination.

Recognition of these laws will be facilitated by a preliminary and thorough investigation of the unit at hand. After asking the *Who*, *What*, *When*, *Where*, *How* and *Why* questions, begin reading through the list of structural laws and ask yourself which can be legitimately identified in the passage. Frequently you will think you have found several. Write them all down and begin reducing them to a manageable number to be considered more seriously. From there, whittle your list down to the three to five that dominate. Finding these laws will challenge the beginner, but regular practice bears fruitful dividends.

The next chapter will investigate interpretation of the structural laws found in Scripture, demonstrating further benefits of their identification and application.

Remember "As-a-whole"

Within any single book, numerous uses of almost all the laws can be found if one forces the process. Keep in mind that the unit you are studying should be considered "as-a-whole." Finding the dominant or primary laws as they relate to the entire unit is a more significant exercise than simply identifying as many laws as possible.

In Ephesians 2:11-22, for instance, the law of comparison is operative in the second chapter where Paul compares believers to a "new man," "fellow citizens," a "household" and the "whole building." Comparison is an important law when considering that unit. When considering the larger unit of Ephesians-as-a-whole, however, the law of comparison as found specifically in Ephesians 2 is not primary.

Suffice it to say that the best way to study a book is to survey and observe the book-as-a-whole first and then survey/observe the major parts-as-a-whole, as major divisions within the book are identified. Your chart for the book of Ephesians should note the major book-as-a-whole structural laws as well as the major subsection laws. Try to identify one major law per unit—one for the entire book-as-a-whole and one for each subsection. These won't be all the important laws you find, but for simplicity's sake on the chart, they should provide important markers for future reference.

Ephesians: Christ and His Church

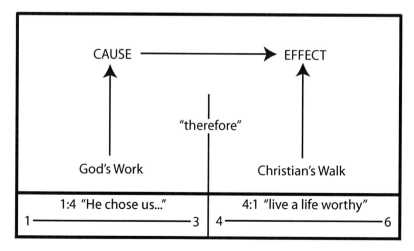

Genesis: "These are the Generations..."

INTERROGATION (PROBLEM/SOLUTION)	
Problem: Sin and Judgment →	Solution: The Covenant

RECURRENCE OF CONTRAST				
Cain ↕ Abel	Noah ↕ Public	Abram ↕ Lot	Jacob ↕ Esau	Joseph ↕ Brothers

REPETITION OF BIOGRAPHIES				
Adam	Noah	Abraham	Jacob	Joseph
1—5	6—10	6—25	26—36	37—50

With charts like these, a glance even months or years after your study will give you a good idea about the message and intention of the book and its divisions.

Watch for Interrelationships and Combinations

A frequent problem in a budding working relationship with the structural laws is the dilemma of "Is it that law? Or that one? Or both?" Struggling mightily between the choices of laws is the essence of growing in expertise with these tools. But, it should be noted that sometimes several laws are operative *in tandem*. For instance, it is possible to see a recurrence of contrast subsequently recognized as "contrast with interchange." Laws can and sometimes need to work together in association.

In Ephesians, Paul begins the fourth chapter by imploring the saints in Ephesus to *"live a life, then, that lives up to the calling of God of which you are already well aware."* The "then" in that verse ties all that follows to Paul's "imprisoned" testimony in the preceding chapter and suggests "cause-effect." The "living up to your calling" ties that verse and all that follows with the first and second chapter of Ephesians. So, the operative structural law becomes "causal comparison." Sounds a bit complicated to the uninitiated, but this is the key to the book of Ephesians. To miss this key is to miss insights into what Paul is trying to relate in that short epistle.

The confidence that would allow this kind of accurate and refined analysis comes only with practice. And, if it would assuage the reader's feelings of possible inadequacy at this point, reputable scholars can look at a single book or passage and come up with different opinions as to its structural makeup. Varying perspectives aside, the beauty of the structural laws is that a much simpler rendering of the compositional relationships within Ephesians or any other book is possible, often enabling impressive insights. Arriving at an educated presumption of certain structural laws after serious reading and consideration will allow the student to see the unit with fresh understanding and renewed interest.

As Robert Traina relates in *Methodical Bible Study*, contrast frequently accompanies interchange, particularization and summarization have much in common, and on it goes. The authors of this text, having studied under Traina, have seen the professor combine structural laws with such confidence that we have cowered in the insecurity that such answers could ever arise from our own work.

Nonetheless, we should plunge in. Even Traina suggests that differences of opinion can arise and subjective analysis is necessary. The point is that with practice and good faith application of the laws, expertise will grow and the Bible will begin opening up to the student of Scripture as it never has before. Furthermore, if instead of the "law of causal comparison" a student simply finds "cause-effect" or "comparison", the accrued benefit is substantial and much can be legitimately learned. Seminary professors find great gain in poring over Scripture to determine structural laws, and the writers of this text know elementary school-aged children who have begun to recognize them in various passages.

> Note that as with many newly acquired skills, the more you engage a discipline the more the discipline becomes at once both easier and more complex. The "easy" part comes because practice with the laws obviously facilitates their use. The "complicated" part indicates that, as with almost every other endeavor worth mastering, the more one discovers the more one needs to learn. In other words, the use of the structural laws of composition is far more like chess than checkers—it can get complicated. But few people who have arrived at even an elementary level of chess ever goes back to checkers.

Find the Strategic Areas

Once a few primary structural laws are recognized in the text, it is beneficial to highlight key verses associated with those laws which provide windows of insight into the unit's interrelationships. If the law of cruciality/pivot is operative, identify several verses that emphasize the pivotal moment. These key verses serve as markers that summarize the book's major movements. When making a chart for the book we normally cite the strategic verses in prominent display on the page with a brief reference to the structural law(s) involved.

To communicate the message of the book of Ruth, one might recount from the first five verses how miserable life had become for the women featured in that account. The last several verses comprise the climax. The reader is left to judge where the pivotal point comes in the middle of the text. (Go ahead, see if you can find it!) Wherever this pivot takes place, these three passages constitute the strategic verses of Ruth and are therefore important to the communication of its message.

It could be fairly suggested that I Kings 11:1-13 (the folly of Solomon) contains the strategic verses for both I and II Kings. Before these verses, there is promise and God's blessing. After these verses, with rare exception, come tragic leadership and unfortunate national consequences. As another example, in Ephesians, strategic verses might include 1:1-14 (preparatory material and significant recurrences) and 4:1 (comparison and clear cause/effect cues). Using these two strategic areas for further study would be profitable for communication of the "big ideas" of this epistle. When presenting biblical truth, a verse-by-verse synopsis may occasionally be appropriate. But the "strategic verse" approach frequently provides a more effective way to convey the sweep of history or ideas with more focused attention to the text.

Dennis Kinlaw, former president of Asbury College, recounts this remembrance of his Princeton professor, Otto Piper: The professor used to chide learners in the lecture hall for underlining verses in their Bibles. It was not, declared Piper, their role to decide which passages were more important than others by underlining some and not others. Piper had a point. Strategic verses aren't selected because they are more important than any of the rest of the unit. They are selected because they open windows of understanding to the rest of the book or section via the recognition of the structural laws.

Remember, the first major step of inductive Bible study, after prayer, is observation. Missionary E. Stanley Jones once said that no person can be spiritual who is not scriptural. If there is dust on your Bible, he said, there is dust on your experience with God. Ardent observation is an excellent way to wipe away the dust and get serious with God and His revelation to us. Reading and rereading, asking questions and searching for structural laws are some of the best ways to examine what the writers of the sacred text were attempting to communicate then and what God through that Word is trying to communicate now.

THE STRUCTURAL LAWS: A Summary

- **Repetition:** The law of repetition connotes repeated use of a word, phrase or idea.

- **Preparation/Introduction:** This law signifies that the reader is being prepared for what follows through background information or the setting of events/ideas.

- **Comparison:** The law of comparison is the comparing of similar things to demonstrate likeness.

- **Contrast:** The law of contrast is also a comparison of dissimilar things in order to highlight differences.

- **Climax:** The law of climax follows a gradual progression to the high point of a unit.

- **Continuation:** The law of continuation signifies the extended treatment of a subject and the carrying through to completion of an idea or series of events. It involves extension, rather than merely recurrence.

- **Cruciality/Pivot:** The law of cruciality or pivot is seen during narrative units when a definite turn of events takes place.

- **Interchange:** The law of interchange, a subsidiary law, utilizes alternating elements which frequently strengthen contrasts and comparisons.

- **Particularization/Generalization**: The law of particularization is the movement from a general statement to particular ones. The law of generalization is the movement from the particular statements to the general.

- **Cause and Effect**: The law of causation is the presentation of a cause and a notable result.

- **Analysis**: The law of analysis is an event or idea followed by its interpretation.

- **Interrogation**: The law of interrogation is the setting forth of a question or problem and its answer.

- **Harmony**: The law of harmony is a law of connected or completed truth; for instance, promise-fulfillment or disease-remedy.

- **Summarization**: The law of summarization restates the main points before or after a unit of Scripture.

CHAPTER 5

Interpretation

C.S. Lewis once lamented in a letter that the less the Bible is read, the more it is translated. And, he could have added, interpreted. Today it is common to hear, "But, that's *my* interpretation" or "That's just *your* interpretation," concerning Sacred Writ. Sadly, much of that interpretation is built on poor or inadequate reading of the Bible and not on the earnest observation that is central to the inductive process.

Those who attempt to interpret Scripture without carefully reading it commit a grave error. But the error is made by many would-be Bible students who brush off seemingly elementary steps of Bible study in the rush to state what the Bible means on a particular topic or teaching. Suffice it to say, the process of observation as reviewed in the previous two chapters is crucial to the task of interpretation. After the survey of the book has been made and structural relationships have been identified to enable the student to explore section by section, unit by unit, chapter by chapter, paragraph by paragraph and verse by verse—only then can a thorough attempt at interpretation begin.

Once it is surmised that something important is being said, the natural inclination is to consider, "What is *really* being said?" and, "*Why* is this being said?" Interpretation, the next step of Bible study, is the determination of the meaning and significance of a unit of study and its parts. It comprises the asking of probing questions and the process of coming to responsible conclusions. In other words, "What does the text mean?"

Bible study is essential to understanding the Persons of God, the will of God, the lifestyle that is ordered by this will and communicating these perspectives to others. How is this best achieved? A clue from the life of Jesus might be appropriate. Scripture recounts that at the age of twelve the young Savior, absent from His parents, was found in the temple sitting among the teachers, listening and asking questions. From this posture of *inquiry*, Jesus amazed those present with his answers. But mark it well—questions first, then, amazement at answers proffered.

One of Michelangelo's mottos was reportedly *Ancora imparo* or, *"I am still learning."* He possessed an incredible mind, seemingly ahead of his time intellectually. A significant factor in his brilliance was his attitude.

We might assume that if the student of Scripture is willing to assume the posture of learner as did Jesus and Michelangelo, incisive life conclusions and their effective communication are far more likely to follow.

This chapter briefly investigates the tandem practice of asking good questions and arriving at well-reasoned answers. While questions and answers are useful in the observational phase of inductive Bible study, interrogation continues its vital role in the interpretation stage as well.

Hilda Taba, in her research on inductive thinking, called this stage of induction the process of *making inferences*. That means, of course, seriously considering the message of the text but also going beyond what was given in the words of the text. It comprises finding implications, extrapolating data and eliciting questions such as: What does this mean? What picture does it create in your thinking? What would you conclude? Good questions for Taba always preceded the earnest search for answers, and such a search would result in well-deserved findings.

The process of informed inference and drawing of well reasoned conclusions is the nature of interpretation. This is not to suggest, of course, that the Bible becomes less important in interpretation than in the step of observation simply because Taba and others suggest "going beyond" the text. But it does allow God to use the creative minds and imaginations He has given His people.

Be Clear on Your Passage Size

Make sure you know how large or small your unit is before the interpretive process begins. If your "unit" is the first chapter of Ephesians, for instance, the questions will differ from those asked if your "unit" were the entire epistle of Ephesians. With a single chapter or paragraph, inquiries are applied to a far more concentrated section and the time spent in investigation is far more intense and specific than when dealing with a larger unit. On the other hand, a bird's eye interrogation takes the questioning process to another level that offers a different, more generalized but hardly inferior, perspective.

Turn Questions on Each Other

Chapter three recommended the frontline questions of good reporting: *Who? What? When? Where? How?* and *Why?* But rather than stopping there, a further technique might be found profitable.

- Instead of just asking *Who*, ask *What, When, Where, How* and *Why* inquiries of the answers to the *Who* questions.

- And *Who, What, Where, How* and *Why* of the answers to the *What* questions.

- And *Who, What, Where, How* and *Why* of the answers of the *When,* questions. And so on.

Here's how it works: After applying the *Who* questions suggested in chapter three and finding some preliminary, albeit simple, answers, let's investigate how some of the other questions could be "turned on" the *Who* answers.

Who wrote the epistle of Ephesians? Paul, an apostle of Jesus Christ. To whom? To saints who are at Ephesus. With those two questions and textually sound answers, turn the other questions on the *Who* inquiry. Here are some examples:

What is an apostle? What does the name "Paul" mean? What is a saint? What difference did Jesus make in Paul's testimony?

When did Paul live? When did Paul write this letter?

Where was Paul when he wrote the letter? Where did Paul become an apostle? Where is Ephesus? Where did the saints read the epistle?

How did Paul become an apostle? How does Paul's linkage to Jesus Christ validate his letter? How does one earn the name "saints?"

Why, in light of who Paul is, is a letter from Paul necessary? Why does Paul link himself with Jesus? Why is he writing to the church at Ephesus? Why does the writer call these people "saints"?

If this process of "turn-about" questioning continues, you could, from only the first verse of Ephesians, easily come up with a hundred questions. Arduous investigation of the answers to these questions, or even a few of them, will lead to principles and lessons that can and should be implemented by the practicing Christian.

*Arrival at such teachable principles is the heart of interpretation—*asking the initial six categories of questions, turning those questions on each other and then searching for meaning and significance. It becomes a natural process after much practice. Some of the best illumination of the Word comes in simply bandying about a verse in group study, listening to a teacher present material or hearing a pastor's sermon.

Choose Questions To Answer

As questions multiply, it will soon become obvious that not all of them can be answered. If a hundred or more questions could be asked about a single verse, then it stands that progress in Bible study will be extremely slow if a thorough study is desired. The dilemma in Bible study is the *same problem that faces us in life—which questions will we spend time answering?* You can't answer them all in depth. So, choosing which questions are of interest to you, most critical to understanding the unit at hand, most relevant to the devotional life and of import to the teaching task ahead is a critical part of the interpretation process.

Some scholars literally spend a lifetime in the study of primarily one book. The best of these scholars consciously ask basic questions and fulfill their vocational call to seek answers to what generalists would deem mere nuances. To such scholars we must remain grateful, for their work furthers the Church's knowledge base and opens minds to Scripture. But since time is of the essence in most cases, students of the Bible will find a less exhaustive approach necessary if the objective is communication of the full counsel of Scripture.

These basic questions are a perfect start. Pick a few inquiries that in your judgment get to the essence of the message, and begin exploring for the answers. Out of the questions just covered it would be reasonable, after examining the full course of possibilities, to settle on a few and prepare for the next step in the process.

When answering questions, it is vital to employ sound principles of interpretation. Following are some that should help guide the way:

a. Remember context! Traina, in *Methodical Bible Study*, calls fragmentary interpretation one of the most grievous errors to be made in Bible study. And, he says Christian ministers should be ranked among the worst offenders. To cite a scriptural quotation as a text and then completely ignore the setting of that verse or pericope, is poor treatment of God's Word. When interpreting a passage, the Bible itself should be used as the primary reference source for, as the Reformation fathers noted, sacred Scripture is its own interpreter. Conclusions drawn from one section of the Bible ought to be consistent with the whole counsel of Scripture and congruity should be sought. The first wave of illumination in interpretation ought to come from the Source itself. Again, *let Scripture interpret Scripture*. Every word, every verse, every teaching must be examined in the light of the surrounding passage, of the book which contains it and, ultimately, in light of the whole Bible.

This contextual principle of interpretation should be understood with a degree of *time sensitivity*. The Bible normally means what its most apparent reading would suggest. But it should be remembered that an interpreter of Scripture seeks primarily to understand what the author intended when he wrote the words. Since the author lived in a different era, context again becomes all-important because what was meant then by a word, a phrase, a story or even a structural law may be something slightly or even very different than what is meant in our contemporary period. A contextual approach that gains perspective over a lifetime of study should be the long-term aim.

b. Remember figures of speech! Figurative language must be recognized and respected in the process of interpretation. In Luke 22:19, for example, Jesus offers bread to his disciples in the upper room at the Last Supper, telling them that this is His body. The interpretation of this text rests on whether one does or does not determine this to be a metaphor. If so, the bread is a symbol for Jesus' body. If not, the bread *is* his body (from whence comes the doctrine of transubstantiation).

Figures of speech are often used in great literature because they bring a sort of illumination or insight to the reader. These devices help to clarify meaning or reveal truth in a more dramatic way. The Bible is no exception. Following is a list of a few figures of speech and examples of them from Scripture:

- **Metaphor:** an implied comparison in which words of comparison (*like, as, as such*) are not used because the thing spoken of is used as if it were that different thing. For instance, in the "armor of God" passage in Ephesians 6, the sword of the Spirit *is* the Word of God (verse 13).

- **Simile:** an obvious comparison utilizing the words *like, as* and *as such* where the comparison is openly stated. In Mark 4:30, for instance, Jesus says that the Kingdom of God is *like* a mustard seed.

- **Hyperbole:** purposeful exaggeration to emphasize a point. In Matthew 9:47, Jesus emphasizes that if your eye causes you to sin, pluck it out. To recognize this hyperbole and the truth behind it in Matthew results in great profit spiritually. To miss the device means bodily harm and irresponsible communication. Hyperbole is usually easy to spot but is occasionally debatable.

- **Synecdoche:** words denoting the whole refer to the part or words denoting the part refer to the whole. Throughout Scripture the term "law" is used. It may refer to the entire Old Testament, to the Pentateuch, or more, specifically, to the Ten Commandments.

- **Irony:** an expression stating the direct opposite of what is intended is stated. In I Kings 22, Micaiah tells the king with a sarcastic tone what the king wants to hear. The irony is so obvious that even the king picks up on it.

Although this is by no means an exhaustive list (and some figures of speech like alliteration, assonance and onomatopoeia, show up only in the original languages), the above types predominate and give the student of Scripture significant assistance in the discipline of interpretation.

c. Remember genre! Literary style will at times influence interpretation. Obviously, there are more metaphors, similes, and personification in the wisdom literature. You will observe more emotional emphasis and passion in books of poetry and prophecy as compared to historical narratives and biographies. Proverbs, for instance, includes maxims that are generally true for life. They are not meant to be absolute promises for all people at all times, nor are they prophetic in nature. Consideration of the genre, then, is a significant step in interpreting the meaning of Scripture.

Interpretive Questions with the Structural Laws

The following constitute recommended reportorial questions once the structural laws are recognized. These queries will work in nearly all cases. Other *who/what/when/where/how/* and *why* questions should be considered on a case-by-base basis:

Preparation/Introduction:
- *What* is meant by the preparatory words?

- *What* is the author trying to establish with the introductory statement?
- *How* does the material in the unit prepare for what comes after?
- *Why* did the author use this preparatory movement?
- *What* are the overall implications of its use?

Recurrence:
- *What* does the repeated element mean?
- *What* are the different ways the recurring element is used?
- *What* are the full implications of the author's recurrent use?

Comparison:
- *What* is the meaning of each of the persons, places or things being compared?
- *What* is the similarity(s) between them, and what is the meaning of this similarity(s)?
- *Why* is/are the similarity(s) stressed by the author?
- *What* are the full implications of the comparison(s)?

Contrast:
- *What* is the meaning of each of the contrasting persons, places or things?
- *What* is the difference(s) between them, and what is the meaning of this difference(s)?
- *Why* is the difference(s) stressed?
- *What* does it imply?

Climax:
- *What* is the meaning of the high point of the unit being studied?
- *How* do the preceding materials lead to this high point?
- *Why* does the author use this climactic movement and that which leads up to it?
- *What* are the full implications of the use of climax here?

Continuation:
- *What* is the subject that the author feels compelled to continue discussing?

- *What* is the importance of this topic?
- *Why* is the law of continuation used?
- *Why* is the law of continuation used here?
- *What* is implied by its usage?

Cruciality/Pivot:
- *What* is the meaning of the pivotal movement? How does it serve to change the direction of the unit?
- *How* does what precedes lead to the climax, and how does what follows flow from it, to affect the use of the crucial moment/teaching?
- *Why* does the author use the law of cruciality?
- *What* is implied by its use?

Interchange (secondary law used to augment a primary relationship):
- *What* is meant by each of the alternating elements?
- *Why* does the author use interchange to strengthen his point?
- *What* are the full implications of the use of interchange?

Particularization/Generalization:
- *What* is the meaning of the general statement and of the particular statement(s)?
- *How* does the general statement illuminate the particular statement(s), and *how* does the particular statement(s) illuminate the general statement?
- *Why* use such particularization/generalization?
- *What* does it imply?

Cause and Effect (or vice versa):
- *What* is meant by the cause?
- *What* is meant by the effect?
- *How*, specifically, does the cause result in the effect?
- *Why* did the author use this causal movement?

Analysis:
- *What* is being analyzed?
- *What* are the critical points of the analysis?

- *How* does the analysis bring clarity to the topic?
- *Why* is the law of analysis necessary at this point?
- *What* does the use of analysis imply?

Problem/Solution:
- *What* does it imply of the question (problem) and of the answer (solution)?
- *How* does the answer (solution) resolve the question (problem)?
- *Why* use the law of interrogation?
- *What* are its full implications?

Summarization:
- *What* is the meaning of the summary statement?
- *How* does it summarize the materials involved?
- *Why* such summarization?
- *What* is implied by it?

Harmony:
- *What* is it that the author is bringing into harmony?
- *How* do the elements of the harmony strengthen the message of the author?
- *Why* did the author use the law of harmony?
- *What* are the full implications of its use?

Here is an example of some preliminary answers to one group of these questions. Since cause/effect is paramount in the book of Ephesians, we will probe these questions in brief. A lengthier and more thorough pursuit of the questions could obviously be attempted.

Example of Answers to Interpretive Questions of the Ephesians Causal Movement

What is meant by the *cause*? The cause in Ephesians-as-a-whole is contained in chapters 1-3. In 4:1, Paul urges the Ephesians to live a life worthy of their calling which is seen in those first three chapters. Paul writes first of the spiritual blessedness of the Ephesians (1:3-14):

- how they were chosen to be holy
- blameless
- adopted as one of the sons of Jesus
- recipients of redemption
- made for the praise of His glory
- marked with the Holy Spirit

In other strategic passages of the first three chapters, Paul describes the Ephesians as

- made alive in Christ (2:4-5)
- works of art for God and for service (2:1-10)
- one of the promised people, as Gentiles, with Israel (2:11-22)
- preached to and prayed for by Paul, the apostle who was given a special administration of God's grace to go to these Ephesian gentiles (3:1-21)

All of these ten notable blessings from the first chapters of Ephesians carry with them a sudden responsibility as expressed in 4:1: live a life worthy of your chosenness, your blamelessness, your adoption and your salvation gift, as well as of your destiny in God's exaltation. Your lifestyle must be worthy of your marking with the Holy Spirit, your aliveness in the risen Christ and the work God has planned for you in His service. Obvious questions for further teaching opportunities are: What does it mean to live a life worthy of "chosenness" or "blamelessness," or of being marked with the Holy Spirit, etc.?

What is meant by the *effect*? The "effect" in Ephesians-as-a-whole is found substantially in chapters 4-6.

- *There should be unity in the Body of Christ* while recognizing the diversity of gifts God has given to his various people for the work of ministry and the maturation of His people (4:1-16).

- There ought to be a *putting off* of the "old self"—no longer walking like those alienated from God *but putting on* the new person: living a life of true righteousness and holiness, putting away lying and needless anger, working and not stealing, incorporating a graceful tongue, putting away all forms of evil and being kind to one another (4:17-32).

- *Be imitators of God* and walk in love—not allowing fornication, uncleanness, covetousness, foolish talking and the like being named among us (5:1-7).

- *Walk in the light*, not in darkness—have no fellowship with unfruitful works of darkness (expose them!), walk circumspectly, redeem the time, understand the will of the Lord, be not drunk with wine, be filled with the Spirit, make melody in your hearts and with tongues, give thanks and submit to one another (5:8-21).

- *Wives submit/husbands love* as Christ loved the church and as they love their own bodies. Children obey parents, fathers do not provoke children to wrath, servants be obedient to masters and serve as to the Lord, not men. Masters, treat your servants with respect and with the Master in mind (5:22-33).

- *Put on the armor of God.* Pray for the Body, and for me, Paul (6:10-24).

How, specifically, does the cause result in the effect? Paul's substantial challenges in chapters 4-6 appear for a simple reason demonstrated in chapters 1-3: the Ephesians' calling is extraordinary. In light of the supernatural calling placed on the lives of the saints in Ephesus much is required. But the challenges of the last three chapters are not intended to be laborious and difficult. Indeed, the Ephesians were made for these kinds of behaviors. It is the way that an adopted, predestined, redeemed, alive, unified spirit-filled Christian is programmed to live. Even so, there are other things to keep in mind, most notably, the fact that an enemy is on the loose, and the spiritual battle that is raging.

Why did the author use this causal movement? Paul apparently wants to challenge the believers in Ephesus to new heights. He employs classic communication strategy, encouraging them by making them conscious of their standing in Christ and then by telling them about the implications of that standing. It is an encouraging and challenging letter. As a useful tactic for Christian leadership, we would do well to keep in mind that an encouraging tone and reminders of blessedness are a good initial strategy for subsequent imperatives for better living.

Since you will certainly want to refer to your notes in the future on a passage, it is always good to develop lists and charts when recording answers. They will provide easy recall of principles in a usable form for future lesson material.

As with the more basic questions, choosing where to expend time and studious energy is one of the most important interpretive decisions you will make. But just as the use of structural laws has been offered as a step beyond the more fundamental questions, the use of the questions that accompany these laws is another phase of inductive Bible study that will significantly enrich the learning process. Plumbing the depths of selected inquiries that attend the laws of composition will lead to a deeper understanding of Scripture.

Bible First, Then Other Scholars

In the interpretive process, the Biblical text itself receives the primary and most intensive attention. The immediate biblical context should be examined (i.e., the data that can be observed in the unit) and then the broader context surrounding the unit being studied (chapter, section, book, related books, the broader data contained in the entire Scripture). Once interpretive questions are posed, however, and the answers from the context appropriately examined, the work of other scholars may provide beneficial insights.

The problem inherent in utilizing the work of other scholars is that it becomes the easy first stop in Bible study rather than the final phase of the process. If the scholarly "helps" are consulted too quickly, the learner is cheated in the learning process, for learning worked out for oneself is always more intellectually indelible and affectively appreciated. Also, too many insights are likely to be missed if one's own effort is discounted. Many biblical scholars, for instance, won't suggest to their readers the literary laws inherent in the text. If the learners don't figure it out by themselves, the text probably won't receive sufficient attention to provide adequate knowledge of the unit under study.

If the observation and interpretation steps that precede the perusal of the work of other scholars are done thoroughly and well, then surveying other outstanding resources is not only appropriate, but also will heighten the impact of firsthand study. The list at the end of this chapter suggests resources that we would recommend for the serious pursuer of Scriptural truth.

Interpretation out of subjective bias should be called ventriloquism. Scripture only appears to be speaking. In reality it is your own voice coming through. Skipping observation and proceeding to interpretation is like talking without knowing what you are saying. The serious student of Scripture should aim for certain knowledge and communication of truth from the text, plain and simple.

CHAPTER 6

Correlation

John Wesley wanted to be known as a *Bible bigot*, a man of one Book who used it for the total ordering of his life. But he was also one of England's most widely read individuals and wrote broadly on numerous political, social, health, and religious issues. To say that he was a "man of one Book" does not imply that the Bible was the only volume he ever read or appreciated, but for Wesley, Scripture came first.

Similarly, Scripture should be the Christian believer's primary source of truth. However, the correlation component of inductive Bible study recognizes the value of portions of the Bible other than the specific section under study, as well as extra-biblical data and experience. ***Correlation is, in short, the examination of relevant data from other biblical passages, from history, and from life experiences.*** Correlation is the next to last step in a four-step inductive process, and its goal mirrors the overall objective of inductive Bible study: building a vital and relevant Biblical theology which will affect one's world view, philosophy of life and pattern of daily living.

To arrive at this theology one must, through correlation, find comparisons and contrasts with the data in other scriptural passages. Discovering this interconnectedness is one of the most exciting parts of the inductive process. But the person engaged in inductive Bible study also seeks to understand how the scriptural data found and interpreted connects with contemporary events; the lives of saints in previous ages; the history of one's locale, one's country and the world; the ongoing experience of one's audience. Moreover, we include whatever sources of data the faithful Christian comes into contact with in the normal activity of life.

Correlation occurs naturally as one proceeds through the observation and interpretation processes. As other data comes to mind, keep a notepad handy to record those impressions. Traina suggests in *Methodical Bible Study* that correlation is as much an attitude as it is a step in the procedure, and the correlative mind finds itself primed to bring scriptural truth to the attention of students with lasting impact.

Correlation is the process of cross-referencing the message already uncovered in Scripture in order to make the truth memorable to students. On a personal level, correlation is the connection of truths that makes the principles as penetrating and replete with meaning as possible.

In some ways, correlation coincides with creative thinking insofar as it allows the scholar to consider ancient, contemporary and personal truths, but in a slightly different way. The student of Scripture must treat the text with deference to the author's intent, while deriving fresh insights or new ways of highlighting the truths discovered. Because we have all encountered different experiences and look at standard data with a different set of mental background and images, fresh insight is not only possible but inevitable. Maximizing this dynamic is the intent of correlation in inductive Bible study.

The correlation process enables more effective communication because it considers not only analytical data but also patterns and pictures. This aspect is important, for as homiletics professor Fred Craddock reminds us, we communicate to people who have daily concrete experiences. No farmer thinks seriously about the problems of calfhood, Craddock contends in *As One Without Authority*. He deals with calves. Hence, if at the end of the inductive Bible study process, the teacher has discovered the serious problem of evil as found in one of the Proverbs, his best bet when communicating that predicament is to:

- find other teachings on evil in Scripture

- recall instances of evil in biblical situations, for example David and Bathsheba

- describe how evil reared its ugly head in the concentration camps of Nazi Germany and/or

- recount how evil tried to insinuate itself into the teacher's life this week—in detail

Not all of these approaches might be appropriate considering the audience and the subject as it pertains to a certain passage. But the point is simple. Correlation brings the possibility of additional data and experience to the matter at hand. To ignore this dynamic is to short circuit the process of informing students in ways by which they will most effectively learn.

In Taba's inductive model, correlation is included in various nuances of interpretation. This occurs as she identifies bits of detail, relates those points to other points and extrapolates the data discovered to other elements not directly present in the passage under investigation. It is the yielding to concentric circles of meaning and appreciation for findings beyond the direct purview of the learner's current biblical study. Correlation becomes, in the specific case of inductive Bible study, both a natural and an intentional broadening of what has been distinctly discovered in the process of Bible study.

One major caution: While different faith traditions may vary as to the role of correlation, as authors it is necessary for us to point out that for us Scripture is always first. Things like reason, experience and tradition should serve, not co-opt, our understanding of that primary source of truth. For us, Scripture is not on equal footing with other sources of truth. It stands above other data that might be used in the correlative dynamic. This is a key hermeneutical point: how one approaches correlation is no minor part of the process. It will make a difference whether you see the Bible as *the* authority, or merely one of many good authoritative options. Again, as authors, it is for us the authority. Scripture first. Reason, experience and tradition can help us to understand what that Word means, but these must bow the knee in reverence to the Book, not vice versa.

In any case, after an objective pursuit of observation and interpretation has been undertaken, consider the following approaches when proceeding to the correlation phase of the inductive process:

Concentric Circles

Explore the concentric biblical circles that emanate from the text being examined. Look at the book-as-a-whole, proceed to the testament-as-a-whole, and eventually to the Bible-as-a-whole. Most frequently the unit being examined is part of a book, and that being the case, the larger context of the book needs to be taken into consideration. The overarching question: Is there data within the rest of the book, the rest of the testament (Old or New) or the rest of the Bible that would elucidate the major findings and principles of the passage under study?

In Ephesians, one of the most well-known passages deals with Paul's illustration of truth, righteousness, peace, faith, salvation and the Word of God. These are associated respectively with a belt, a breastplate, fitted feet, a shield, a helmet and a sword. Correlative question: are there other places in Ephesians where Paul expands upon any of the above elements? The answer is yes. For instance, previously peace has a face—in chapter 2, Christ Jesus is proclaimed as peace personified. Does this correlation help me understand chapter 6 and the armor of God? It should.

Look at the Author-as-a-Whole

If there are other references to peace in Ephesians, does the concept appear in other Pauline epistles, too? Indeed it does. In fact, most Pauline epistles mention the word. Do these occurrences clarify the biblical concept of peace? Most assuredly they will. For instance:

- Disorder is juxtaposed with **peace**. Indeed, God is said to be a God of **peace**; specifically not of disorder or unregulated worship (I Corinthians 14:33).

- **Peace** is said to transcend understanding and is capable of guarding hearts and minds (Philippians 4:7).

- **Peace** is made through the blood of Christ, shed on the cross (Colossians 1:19-20). Reconciliation with God is the essence of that **peace**.

- The **peace** of Christ is to "rule" over all else in our hearts (Colossians 3:15).

- **Peace** comes when our minds are controlled by the Spirit (Romans 8:6). The God of hope that fills us with **peace** (Romans 15:13).

- **Peace** is to be pursued (2 Timothy 2:22).

While not an exhaustive list, the foregoing shows how "peace" and, indeed, any other substantial word in the Bible can be pursued within the context of Scripture and provide substantial insights.

Another example: It is one thing to see the "worthy life" as Paul considers it in Ephesians. But Paul, in writing the epistle, addressed a people facing a different set of circumstances than, say, the church at Corinth. Even so, did Paul discuss "a worthy life" in the two epistles to the Corinthians? Certainly. Comparisons and contrasts found in those epistles and others shed light on one's findings. A simple concordance can be helpful in identifying some of the various citings of critical words.

When considering author-as-a-whole, the genre-as-a-whole should be kept in mind as well. Epistolatary material would be a good starting point if Pauline teaching is the concern. Let's briefly examine "peace" again in epistles written by someone other than Paul:

- **Peace** is linked with holiness, without which no one shall see the Lord. Make every effort, the letter says, to be at **peace** with all men (Hebrews 12:14).

- **Peace** is something to be sure to have with God (Philippians 4:7).

- **Peace**makers who sow in peace reap a harvest (James 3:18).

These nuances add to the rich resource of Pauline material.

Another example: If the preaching and teaching of Jesus is the topic of inquiry, then it would be wise to survey the genre of the gospels. In the Old Testament, prophetic writings and approaches could be compared and contrasted as well as the historical accounts in the Pentateuch and beyond.

Look at the Testament-as-a-Whole

Does what Paul said in Ephesians correlate with what Jesus said in the gospels? Do the writings of Peter enhance or expand upon those of Paul or John? When Moses is characterized as the meekest man on the face of the earth, can earlier or later examples of meekness be found in the Old Testament?

Using the ongoing example of peace, we find that it is a crucial concept throughout the writings in the New Testament. For instance:

- Christ called **peace**makers blessed (Matthew 5:9) which brings them into a familial relationship with God; but He also warned that He didn't come to bring **peace** but a sword (Matthew 10:34).

- **Peace** signifies the coming of Jesus and His guidance in our faith-walk (Luke 1:79).

- **Peace** is the state of being in which we want the returning Lord to find us (Philippians 4:7).

- **Peace** is an Old Testament ideal that is to be sought and pursued (1 Peter 3:11).

Look at the Bible-as-a-Whole

The New Testament, it has been said, is the Old Testament unfolded. The Old Testament, on the other hand, is the New Testament enfolded. There are differences between the two major divisions, but far more similarities and rich connections. For instance, an understanding of the Passover experience dramatically informs Jesus' sacrificial death on the cross as recorded in the four gospels. In Exodus, the blood of the slain lamb rubbed over the doorway of every Israelite home saved each family from losing its eldest son when the angel of death came to slay the Egyptian first-born. Without grasping the Hebrew mindset in its celebration of the Passover, one can not fully rejoice in the saving act of the sacrificial lamb, Jesus, or by extension, later writings on the same subject. In this manner, we comprehend how the understanding of one testament sheds light on the other.

Another example: The book of Joshua mentions seven memorials or monuments that are established as the Israelites conquer the promised land. In Acts we find seven "state of the church" updates, all of them inferring or clearly stating the growth of people and power in the burgeoning Christian movement. Joshua is about possessing the land; Acts is about expanding the Jesus movement into the known geographical world. Do you see correlations here?

When truth is uncovered it ought to be correlated with other similar or divergent lessons in Scripture. In order to study the Bible holistically, *cross-referencing* is absolutely necessary. Scripture does not exhaust any subject in one book, one author, one genre or one testament. The entire Bible must be consulted in order to effectively interpret and correlate.

Cross-referencing is referring to any Scripture which amplifies, enlarges, more clearly defines or illuminates the specific Scripture being studied. A critical tool in this process is an exhaustive concordance, which lists every reference for every word in the Bible. This tool enables the student to locate and then investigate other passages relating to the subject under study. Of course, when checking the cross-referenced passages, care must be taken to research and comprehend the context within which that passage occurs.

We have utilized "peace" in foregoing investigations; looking to the Old Testament we will find ample help. A few examples:

- Gideon builds an altar that declares the Lord is **peace** (Judges 6:24).

- In the "songs of ascent," prayers for **peace** are among the most prominent petitions for the holy city of Jerusalem (Psalms 122:6-9).

- **Peace** is one of God's blessings for Israel's obedience to Him, a respite from evil beasts, swords and enemies (Leviticus 26:6-7).

- Wrath awaits the prophet who says there is **peace**, when there is no **peace** (Ezekiel 13:16).

- The Messiah is said to be **peace** (Micah 5:5).

The Old Testament obviously gives a fuller picture of a Pauline teaching. But here is the necessary reminder: A study of the various instances of "peace" within Ephesians can stand by itself as a lesson on peace for a Sunday school class, small group or congregation. But how the word or concept or situation is dealt with in other Pauline writings, or other non-Pauline epistles, or in the gospels and Acts, or in Revelation, or in the Old Testament, brings necessary data to the investigation if the fullest picture possible is desired. Correlation, then, expands the horizons for the learner and thus constitutes one of the most valuable and interesting exercises in the inductive method.

The example of "peace" on previous pages is a kind of word study approach (and we will take another look at word studies in chapter ten). But concepts can be explored this way, as can character traits, nuances of various structural laws, et cetera. The more one observes and interprets the entire Bible, the more the possibilities open themselves up for inter-biblical correlation.

Look at Life-as-a-Whole

John Stott, in his book *Between Two Worlds*, makes the case that to secede from the world into the Bible is escapism; to leave the Bible unopened and to simply engage life around us is conformity. Both are obvious excesses, and imbalance needs to be avoided.

To this point in the book, immersion in the Word has been the heart of the message. But the correlation phase of Bible study involves finding meaningful connections in the world around us. This includes personal experience, books, print and broadcast media, conversation and relationships with others.

Correlation to the world beyond the study desk is easier if a multitude of colorful experiences populate the imagination of the Bible student. A rule of thumb to consider if religious literature is your favorite reading material: Be sure about a third of your total annual reading is outside of biblical, theological, and religious sources. This is particularly true for people in ministry, who can get caught up in a religious publishing subculture if they are not careful.

Stott recounts being part of a reading group that consisted of some young graduates and professional people who met monthly to discuss both secular and religious books. He vigorously supports the benefit of such interaction. The advantage of clergy and laity working together to enrich perspectives and communication is significant. Small groups and their resulting intellectual and relational benefits should be utilized for inductive Bible study but also for sheer personal enrichment.

The late pastor and author Dr. O. Dean Martin once remarked upon purchasing a biography of famed boxer Muhammad Ali that to effectively communicate with a contemporary audience one should read books that the same audience might want to peruse in their leisure time. Too much time spent in the Bible, St. Augustine, Thomas á Kempis and with contemporary Christian authors can potentially leave a teacher woefully out of touch with the world to which he is trying to communicate.

Now, while that advice is certainly valid, it should be taken with a grain of salt. Christian classics such as those penned by Augustine, á Kempis, Brother Lawrence, William Law, John Calvin, Martin Luther, John Wesley, Dietrich Bonhoeffer and C.S. Lewis (to name a precious few) ought to be read diligently. To drink deeply of these is, as Albert Einstein once suggested, to escape being shortsighted and encased in the contemporary at the expense of the wisdom of classics.

On the other hand, being from the South we also know that an occasional foray into the likes of Southern authors like Eudora Welty, Willie Morris, or John Grisham isn't a bad idea either. From both classic and modern sources come a rich reservoir of teachable concepts and illustrations, and the Christian communicator should pay heed to materials both old and new, sacred and secular. *The old is time tested; the new is where much of the world is today.*

One of the best ways to stay abreast of the community is the local daily newspaper. The newspaper, and national publications as *USA Today*, *The Wall Street Journal* and weekly news magazines, inform the reader about events in his or her city, state and nation as well as the environment, business, crime, politics, religion, births and deaths, humor and various opinions. The local newspaper of any community contains some of the best correlative material available outside the Bible itself. Indeed, famed theologian Karl Barth said that lesson preparation ought to include the Bible in one hand and the newspaper in the other.

The Internet has become a resource that provides everything a newspaper does, and more. Even where local publications are not available, *USA Today* and *The Wall Street Journal* are, along with online versions of many big city dailies, thousands of magazines, millions of web pages and all the major news services. The Internet is for many people an essential tool for keeping current, at a remarkably affordable price. Television and other video resources also represent a vast ocean of potential. All media, however, should be carefully monitored to avoid 1) wasting an inordinate amount of time on that which is insipid or worthless and 2) a detrimental effect on the thought life. With much helpful material available in a variety of forms, proceed with discretion and with biblical instruction as the objective.

The experience of the teacher or the experience of others we know provides ample avenues of correlation with the Bible. Professor and author Richard Foster, in his bestselling volume *Celebration of Discipline*, discusses the discipline of study. Is there a correlating truth in nature, in your personal, family, or neighborhood history, or in relationships at home, at work or at play? Is there something to be gleaned from an experience today, this week, this year? Is there a question that you can ask a doctor, a lawyer, a homeless person, a fast-food worker, a businessman, a person sitting next to you on the bus that will expand avenues of correlation?

The caution at this point is that one not become sidetracked and lose sight of the original goal: applying relevant Biblical truth to life. To stay culturally apprised is important; on the other hand, there is truly nothing more dismaying than to watch the church running after the world, gasping and wheezing for breath, trying to catch up. After the biblical text has been examined and its message uncovered, the world around us ought to be surveyed for avenues of communication—not to set the pace for us.

If a proper balance is held between the Bible (the primary source), responsible scholarship, Christian classics and the perspective of contemporary experience, then an informed life and the opportunity to enliven an informed biblical perspective is possible. Just as a strong Biblical theology sheds light on every issue of life, the issues of life can sharpen our vision to see the truth of Scripture more clearly, hopefully with more relevance, and from a more creative perspective.

We are reminded time and time again that the most

effective communicators in the world today, with only rare exception, are masters at correlating their subject with their audience. One of the best we have heard—a Christian evangelist and author named Dr. Ravi Zacharias—seemingly enjoys weaving a web of confusion that is fascinating to hear but often leaves the listeners wondering where he is headed. One evening he articulated a concept that seemed remote at best, drawing illustrations from Mother Teresa, Adolph Hitler and Bertrand Russell. Then, with a mighty sentence at the end of his message, he pulled all three of the lives together with truth captured from the biblical text, leaving us mesmerized.

It was a memorable teaching moment. But his message remains unforgettable because of its strong correlation, its drawing together of those illustrative elements and his biblical teaching accomplished with skill and force. When listening to the communicator, the audience was challenged intellectually, captivated emotionally and motivated to action. His presentation encapsulated what ought to be a normative experience in a teaching ministry.

To round out this chapter on looking at life as it pertains to correlation, let us consider "peace" and a few possibilities for investigation:

- Ask, how many countries of the world are at war today. Why?

- Query ten people coming out of the grocery store about what the word "peace" means to them. Record the answers.

- Historically, who are the persons we associate with the word peace? Why?

- How do the sayings in the average book of quotations at the library size up with the biblical notion of peace?

- Are there any recent best-selling books or novels that deal with the topic of peace? Why? Why not?

Exercises like these provide endless possibilities to allow the biblical concepts to interact with the world. As we shall see in the application and presentation phases of inductive study, it is a step that can invigorate the thought life and teaching style of the educator.

CHAPTER 7

Application

Years ago the *Wall Street Journal* featured an article examining the perceived burgeoning interest in religion in this nation. The first subtitle, however, was most disturbing. It went something like this: "A Revival is Sweeping the Nation, But With Little Effect." The last subtitle suggested why: "Shying From Involvement." Christian people need to keep in mind that the strength of inductive Bible study doesn't lie in the vast number of new insights gleaned; it is in exercising the discovered truth. "Revival" without measurable effect and righteous involvement is not viable.

With inductive Bible study, the methodology described to this point will provide means to significantly improve biblical aptitude and to foster a meaningful connection between knowledge and life experience. It involves, as a point of fact and faith, taking seriously God's perspective on life's issues. As *Isaiah* reminds us, God's thoughts are higher than our thoughts. His way of doing things is higher than ours.

It could be said then that *Bible study should have three great ends in mind:*

- *finding out who God is and what He thinks,*

- *finding out what He wants us to do concerning who He is and what He thinks and*

- *doing it.*

Faith, says the book of James, is simply dead without works.

> *What good is it, my brothers, if a man claims to have faith but has no deeds? Can such faith save him? . . . . faith by itself, if it is not accompanied by action, is dead.* (NIV, James 2:14, 17)

But frankly, James was only picking up on a biblical admonition that was a major emphasis of Jesus:

> *Not everyone who says to me, "Lord, Lord," will enter the kingdom of heaven, but only he who does the will of my Father who is in heaven.* (NIB, Matthew 7:21)

> *"For I was hungry, and you gave me nothing to eat, I was thirsty and you gave me nothing to drink, I was a stranger and you did not invite me in, I needed clothes and you did not clothe me, I was sick and in prison and you did not look after me. . . . I tell you the truth, whatever you did not do for one of the least of these, you did not do for me." Then they will go away to eternal punishment, but the righteous to eternal life.* (NIV, Matthew 25:42-43, 45-46)

> *"Who are my mother and my brothers?" he asked. Then he looked at those seated in a circle around him and said, "Here are my mother and my brothers! Whoever does God's will is my brother and sister and mother."* (NIV, Mark 3:33-35)

"Doing" was important to Christ. A Christianity that was grounded cognitively but not behaviorally was hardly the direction of this Rabbi. He taught his disciples *with* activity and *for* activity. He fully anticipated that His kingdom movement would be one of doing the will of God, not just talking about it or merely believing in it. And lest His disciples miss the point, His most thundering warnings about heaven and hell seemed to be with the behavioral component in mind as demonstrated with at least a couple of foregoing Scriptures.

Many key thinkers have picked up on this emphasis of Scripture. The "Disturbing Dane," Soren Kierkegaard, warned against the schoolboy temptation of copying the answer to the quiz out of the textbook without having worked the sum for oneself. For the practitioner of inductive Bible study, working through the observation, interpretation and correlation stages will challenge the student to engage the text. The next step, application, is the process of discovering what God wants us to do with what we have comprehended from Scripture. *The application phase moves from the text to the world.*

Application ought to answer some important questions in the life of educators and those whom they teach:

- Does what I have studied have timeless relevance and is it applicable to modern life?

- By what principles should the Christian believer adapt and alter his/her life?

- With what principles should disciples be challenged in light of the truths discovered by their teacher?

This chapter addresses these considerations.

Application rounds out the observation/interpretation/correlation process of truth inquiry. At its most basic level, it is wrestling with "What do I do now?" Application is frequently the forgotten step of the inductive method. Once truth is grasped intellectually, too many scholars want to move on to the next truth without embracing the Hebraic concept of knowing, that is, to "experience" and "encounter."

Marvin Wilson, in *Our Father Abraham,* notes that for the Hebrew, to know was to do—to act. The Hebrew word for know (y*ada*) was used in a variety of ways in the Old Testament. The first time it is used is in Genesis 4:1—Adam *knew* Eve. *Yada* conveyed in this verse what it would mean elsewhere; frankly, that to know was to experience or to encounter. In that early point in Genesis, it meant sexual encounter. The word appears in many contexts throughout the Old Testament narrative, poetical offerings, and prophetic writings. At its most profound level it expressed the desire of God that His people would know Him and His way of doing things—not just intellectually, but in a much more intimate and experiential sense. They would see their life at its best when they loved God, interacted with Him, developed an intimacy with Him and acted the way He wanted them to act.

Wilson suggests that the idea of knowledge then embraced the whole personality. Memorization, while important, was hardly the point of learning. Knowledge demanded a response in behavior and morals. It meant to do something, to act, or to apply. More than an exercise of the mind it was the exercise of the head, heart and hand together in the various tasks and demands of life. This Hebraic mindset was fundamental not only for the faithful in the Old Testament, but the early church as well and, more particularly, the Rabbi, Jesus Himself, as He instructed the community of disciples.

A basic modern psychological definition of learning is "changed behavior" which seems to correspond nicely with the Hebraic teaching of knowledge—not just changed thinking, or even changed feeling, but a modification of life activity. If Bible study is to have its maximal effect, it should significantly modify not only our heads, but our hearts and hands as well. In essence, Bible study is not just contemplation of what the inspired text says but how that truth ought to be exercised in life. And in the final analysis, this step of the process can only be truly complete when application isn't merely investigated but enacted. Response is non-negotiable.

Hilda Taba, in her third step of the inductive thinking model of information processing, asserts that the main activities in the application stage are 1) predicting consequences of perceived problems and situations and retrieving relevant data necessary to solving those dilemmas; 2) determining the causal links leading to predictions/ hypotheses; and 3) testing the prediction by applying knowledge. The three questions that correspond, respectively, to these steps are: 1) What would happen if . . . ? 2) Why do you think this would happen? and 3) If verified, what would it take for this to be true in the usual situation?

An evangelistic extrapolation of Taba's third question is an important consideration for a student of Scripture: If verified, what would it take for a learning community to help the general community grasp what we have discovered as a faith-based truth? In short, if it is true and helps us to be God's faithful people, *how can we share with others what has become for us the gospel?*

Categories of Truth

Practitioners of inductive Bible study would do well to recognize the categories of truth and determine which are relevant to practical application in the contemporary moment.

The first category was coined *"restricted truths"* by Robert Traina. When some passages of Scripture (e.g., the Levitical regulations covering priests, sacrifices and annual feasts) are evaluated in light of God's complete revelation including the New Testament, for instance, they will be found restricted in many (but not all) ways when being applied from that era to this one. The pre-prophetic teachings of the Old Testament are to be revered and studied, but some of the particular lessons contained will be found to be restricted to that particular place and time in biblical revelation.

The second category of truth is *"localized truth."* I Corinthians 11:2-16 is an example of a largely localized passage. The main (though not only) point of the passage concerns the covering of the woman's head during public worship. There is something to be learned here, perhaps for all believers, concerning respect for God and each other in worship. Furthermore, part of what Paul is trying to address to the church in Corinth has something to do with Greek culture. But universal truth? Few exegetes in the church today are willing to suggest that this truth taught by Paul is to be universal in actual application.

The third category of truth is the *"universal and timeless truth"* which contains verities applicable to everyone in every age. Most of the Bible fits here. Traina, however, when defining these various categories cautions that great care be taken with the many ramifications and variations inherent in the differentiations. To obfuscate the differences leads to a mishandling of what God intended to communicate to his people in the present age.

Heed the "Heart" Component

We have reiterated that God wants to work in the total person, which might be understood through a *head* to *heart* to *hand* continuum. A key but frequently neglected component to application is the *devotional connection* with what is frequently called our "inner lives." In other words, the goal is to take the findings that have been heretofore discovered in the observation-interpretation-correlation cycle and apply them to our *hearts* in the quietness of personal devotional reading, meditation and prayer. This isn't a divergent path from our behavioral emphasis. It is a necessary partner in changing moral behavior from mere Pharisaical going-through-the motions (something Jesus clearly despised, cf.

Matthew 23) to recognizing the full-orbed Hebraic emphasis of thinking, feeling and doing in a singular stream of life.

Again using Ephesians as a case study, serious Bible students will find that for the application phase to have its greatest effect, it is best to allow the Scripture to seep deep into one's inner life before actually communicating—or applying—the lessons to a group.

Let us draw an example from a recent home cell group meeting. The members were discussing the previous week's study, Ephesians 4:1-6, in which Paul makes the powerful point that the Ephesians were to live a life worthy of the calling they had received. The Bible study leader carefully examined the passage and found that it was intimately connected with Ephesians 1-3. Those chapters describe a life lived to the praise of God's glory; the spiritual blessings in Christ Jesus; reconciliation with Christ and with others beyond our traditional community and, in general, the steps to fulfill God's ultimate objectives.

The Bible study leader's application question captured the heart of the matter: Are you living a life worthy of these things Paul has pointed out for us? What keeps us from living that kind of life? What motivates and enables us to live a life that is humble, gentle, patient, loving and unified?

The group leader, however, decided that before he could pose that question with integrity, it needed to be meditated upon—or spiritually pondered—in his own life. After several days of this kind of scriptural meditation, the answer was simultaneously "yes" and "no." Next question: when the Bible teacher could answer "yes," why was this so? When he had to admit "no," then what kept him from this worthy life of which Paul spoke?

Having gathered answers and assumptions to these questions, the teacher was ready to go. Cogent teaching points, complete with penetrating group questions designed to elicit confession, became a secondary goal. Truth applied internally—with outward implications to the teacher first, then to the group—encompassed for that teacher an approach with educational integrity.

Dawson Trotman, founder of the campus discipleship organization The Navigators, was known for saying that teachers should never teach an inch beyond their own experience. Trotman's words are challenging and should lead us to always remember that *application looks inward first, outward thereafter.* It is an important concept to keep in mind when considering Paul's words to his understudy Timothy:

> *All Scripture is God-breathed and is useful for teaching, rebuking, correcting and training in righteousness, so that the man of God may be thoroughly equipped for every good work.* (I Timothy 3:16-17)

The first person to be rebuked, corrected, trained and equipped is the teacher. Inwardly first . . . . outwardly thereafter. The tendency to talk better than we walk may well be why James reminded us that fewer of us should become teachers knowing that if we become educational communicators we will be judged more strictly (James 3:1). Teaching without introspection and righteous change is bound to disappoint.

Consider the Veerman Model

Author Dave Veerman utilizes a nine-box grid that is most beneficial in taking a message of Scripture from truth to response; from the timeless to the contemporary. Across the top of the grid are listed three considerations:

- People's need/predicament
- God's act/answer
- People's reaction/obedience

APPLICATION

Veerman challenges communicators to consider Scripture in light of these three reflections:

- then (in *past* biblical days),
- now (in the *present*) and
- me (*personally*).

	Applying Biblical Truth		
	People's Need/ Predicament	God's Act/ Answer	People's Reaction/ Obedience
Then (past)			
Now (present)			
Me (personally)			

Using Ephesians and the fact that they were once dead in their sin, let us use the categories of the chart.

- The need/predicament of the Ephesians at one point in their lives was that they were dead in their sin. They followed the ways of the world.

- The need/predicament *now* is that some people are still dead in their sin. The question is—would that be us? If not us, then who? Why?

- More particularly, how does the need/predicament relate to *me*? Am I alive or dead in sin? Or, am I as alive as I should be? Why? Even if I claim to be saved, is sin having a deadening effect on my life? How?

Before we continue, notice what just happened. We took the "people's need/predicament" and carried it progressively from a) then, to b) now, to c) me. This is what we will do with Veerman's other two application points. Next:

- **Then,** God's *act/answer* was that He made the Ephesians alive with Christ by His grace. He seated the Ephesians with Christ that He might show His riches of grace.

- **Now,** God's action/solution is that He wants to make us, and those with whom we come into daily contact, alive by His grace. He wants to show us the riches of His grace and seat us with Christ.

- **Me?** Well, He wants me to know aliveness through Christ and the riches of His grace. Do I experience that spiritual vitality? Is there any sense of death/sin working in my life? *Be specific!*

- **Then,** People's *reaction/obedience* is seen in the inferred Ephesian yieldedness to Christ to make them alive and be shown His riches.

- **Now,** Christ still wants to do that, but how can we yield ourselves, and how can we help others to yield?

- **Me?** Christ wants to make me alive. Has he done that already? If it hasn't happened, why not? If I am mostly alive but sin still deadens my life to some extent, what can I do to eradicate the barrier(s) to God's enlivening grace?

The answers to the inquiries above should provide ample

fodder for meditation and prayer as well as material to correlate with other Scripture and illustrations from your church/group/personal life.

The Veerman model is an excellent tool for moving from Scripture to the contemporary situation and then to personal application. Having already studied the structural laws in this volume, you undoubtedly noticed that the grid is set up with the law of interrogation or problem-solution in mind. But could other structural laws be made to work in a similar paradigm? How about the law of contrast or comparison?

> a. The contrast/comparison then, now and with me.
>
> b. God's point in utilizing that contrast/comparison then, now and with me.
>
> c. The proper response/obedience concerning the contrast/comparison then, now and with me.

Or how about the law of climax on a similar grid:

> a. The climax then, now and with me.
>
> b. How God prepared the people for such a climax then, now (how He is preparing or is seeking to) and with me (how does He want to prepare me for a godly climax)?
>
> c. The people's response/obedience to God's preparation and anticipated "climax" then, now and with me.

The law of cause-effect could be explored similarly:

> a. The cause-effect then, now and with me.
>
> b. How God used the cause-effect then, now and with me.

c. The people's response/obedience then, now and with me.

Other structural laws will be useful on such a grid as will other parts of the observation phase of inductive study. Experiment a little and allow God's Word to move from then to today and from the general to the very personal.

After Application

Having practiced this final step of inductive Bible study, *what are some truths that arise in the light of Scripture from your experience in personal application?* From a scientific method point-of-view, theses are never finally proven until they are tested. Scriptural truth can stand the test of time without human trial/failure. It nonetheless is a wonderful model for the teacher to lead students in actually doing the things that have been instructed and then, having obeyed, moving toward reflection of that response.

Some months before this book was written, members of a Sunday School class taught by Matt talked at length about God's attitude toward the poor and how He wanted His people to respond to their plight. It so happens that Matt lives in the capital city of Mississippi, one of the poorest states in the nation and one of the most impoverished small cities in the country. The group had discussed the problem, but they hadn't acted on it. So, one day after a lesson on Jesus and His movement toward the downtrodden, the class took the application step of raising the money for a family living in sub-standard housing and, then, building a home. The group didn't do this single-handedly, but did arrange for it all to happen and expended a good bit of effort and sweat making sure the house was constructed. That single experience has taught the class much about "walking their talk" and provided a fair number of live illustrations that have been amply utilized by the entire local church when considering future response to human need.

This sort of response ought to be the norm in classes taught by leaders who take seriously inductive Bible study and application. Teaching without application inevitably devolves into what E.M. Forster once called "talkative little Christianity," a pale shadow of the biblically active Christian life of integrity, power and substantial witness.

Utilize Community

A powerful teaching tool is the vision and action of a group working together in the application and practice of new or freshly realized truths. In the previous illustration, it was a Sunday school class that moved to obedience. This isn't the only kind of proper response to the Word of God, but it is too frequently one of the least considered simply because the Western mind has been so trained toward individual responsibility and performance. While individual endeavor shouldn't be discounted, the group always seems to be foremost on the mind of God. "Community" is His nation, the family, and the churches of Paul's epistles. Indeed, God Himself is a community of three—Father, Son and Holy Spirit—moving in concert for the divine purpose of redemption. Made in that Image, we must recognize community response as pleasing in the sight of God and as a means by which we are remade in His holiness.

In his landmark work, *A Rumor of Angels,* sociologist Peter Berger explains a crucial connection between faith and community. Serious Bible study inevitably leads one to think in ways that differ significantly from the norm of surrounding society. But without community support, the force of the dominant culture can eventually overwhelm the minority perspective. As Berger puts it, "deviants" from the norm will need to huddle with a "ghetto" or group of like-minded comrades in order to maintain the "deviance" of their Biblical worldview. That ghetto provides the best chance for Christians to move together and in that togetherness hold each other to our faith. Indeed, a sustained faith movement stands no chance of survival without living, conversing and moving with the like-minded. Is there a reader who wonders about the use of "deviant"? If the Bible doesn't ask us to deviate from current behavior or the norm of culture, then what does it ask us to do?

It is interesting that Ephesians, used repeatedly in this text, contains a clue to this community dynamic. Two words found in this epistle—*sunezoopoiesen* (made alive with/Eph. 2:5) and *sunarmologoumenon* (fit together/Eph. 4:16)—appear nowhere in classical Greek. Dr. Dennis Kinlaw, in his book, *Preaching in the Spirit,* suggests that Paul and other New Testament writers had a problem. They were trying to describe something that had never happened before and it was necessary that they coin a new vocabulary to portray it. These words of Paul, and a handful of others in the New Testament, are called by some *sun-* words (*sun* meaning "with") because of their common prefix in the Greek. The biblical authors were, says Kinlaw, trying to describe a relationship with God and with each other so unlike anything that had happened theretofore in world history that they couldn't help creating new "with-it" words. Obviously this Christianity stands in striking contrast to modern individualism.

This is true not only as theological/cognitive truth, but also as theological/kinesthetic truth, or, simply, truth enacted. Individuals are spiritually healthy only as they learn to apply God's truth. His plan has always been for individuals to operate and apply His revelation of righteousness in the context of community. Indeed, that is how this three-in-one God Himself operates. Discussion and implementation of truths found in inductive Bible study should always at the very least be adopted on an individual basis. But when the community of believers chooses to act together in obedience to God, the effect is multiplied.

In a journal entry, Soren Kierkegaard once wrote about some tame geese who week after week attended church and heard teachings on God's great gift to geese—wings. With wings, the preaching gander reminded them, they could fly and experience the many blessings known only through the utilization of that gift. But, laments Kierkegaard, week after week they waddled home without flapping their way to the flight they were told was their destiny. In a sobering conclusion, Kierkegaard reports that these waddling geese were very well liked by the humans of the land. They grew fat and plump and were then butchered and eaten. And that, says the philosopher, was the end of that.

Lesson? God gives us wings—our imaginations set aloft through inductive Bible study. We observe what God is communicating about how we can be holy as He is holy; we interpret these lessons to find relevance for today; we correlate these lessons to other Scriptures and to life; and we learn what it means to apply these lessons in the everyday comings and goings of our existence. But these wings are designed for more than scintillating lessons that will at least keep our students awake for an hour or so and at most entice them back next week. They are designed to be put into practice. If they are, we will be blessed. And, if they are *not*, it is to our own peril. More than a lesson from Kierkegaard, this is a lesson reiterated throughout the Bible as illustrated in this passage from Deuteronomy (NIV):

> *See, I set before you today life and prosperity, death and destruction. For I command you today to love the Lord your God, to walk in his ways, and to keep his commands, decrees, and laws; then you will live and increase, and the Lord your God will bless you in the land you are entering to possess. But if your heart turns away and you are not obedient, and if you are drawn away to bow down to other gods and worship them, I declare to you this day that you will certainly be destroyed. You will not live long in the land you are crossing the Jordon to enter and possess.* (30:15-18)

What we do with what we know matters.

In the practice of inductive Bible study, the process of application is never completed. Biblical knowledge comprises a lifetime of careful study, earnest understanding, and then heartfelt living out of the lessons contained within.

CHAPTER 8

Character Study

The gospel of Matthew says that before Mary became pregnant an angel spoke to Joseph and revealed that his future bride would soon be with child and that he would be known as Immanuel—*God with us*. The last line of that same gospel showcases Jesus saying something equally as extraordinary—*I am with you always, to the end of the age.*

Jesus is the most fascinating personality in world history because of one major characteristic of His life: He was God in the flesh who embodied God's eternal principles. While orthodoxy confirms that Jesus was a person before He was incarnate, His in-the-flesh character is what emblazoned the God-message in a way that is truly unforgettable and absolutely unique among the world's religions. *At the core of Christianity, then, is the character study:* what it means to be holy as He is holy, and what it means to perfectly personify the very life of the Holy One of Israel. At the core of biblical revelation are the stories of men and women, each embodying messages both positive and negative that when properly understood can be gleaned for great spiritual enlightenment.

Character studies in the Bible highlight people whose stories we can relate to and from whom we can learn. And in an empathetic sense, that is what is so compelling about studying the attributes of historic characters. With rare exception, biblical persons are so much like us: capable of extraordinary successes and phenomenal failures; of both rejoicing and weeping; and of noble feats as well as dastardly deeds. We can read, relate and choose to emulate or repudiate.

The possibilities for inspiration are ample, since Scripture contains a bit less than three thousand names. Some of the individuals are only mentioned. Other people's lives, like David's, are chronicled in substantial detail. And what is interesting about someone like King David is that he is mentioned around fifty times in the New Testament as well. In addition, the story of his life and times can be followed in four historical books of the Old Testament and can be traced through over seventy psalms. A fairly extensive character analysis can therefore be conducted on this son of Jesse, King of Israel, and notable entry in the lineage of Jesus.

But a character study can also be done using Shamgar, one of the judges of Israel, whose account consists of twenty words, one comma and two periods. David was a major player on the Israelite scene. Shamgar, given the brief testimony of Scripture regarding him, was hardly more than a minor footnote. And yet a profitable examination can be made of both men. With inductive Bible study, both character studies would include the same basic pattern covered heretofore: examining the details of the scriptural data on the men; asking and seeking answers to key questions; correlating information gleaned elsewhere in the Bible as well as from extra-Biblical literature and then applying principles learned.

Looking at the personalities of Scripture is a part of the inductive Bible study process in several ways. Regular studies of their lives provide fodder for continued correlation at a later date and, secondly, the most powerful illustrations of scriptural truths are imbedded in their lives. Also, while the character study is not necessarily a step unto itself in the procedure of inductive Bible study, a steady diet of personalities paraded before our own hearts and minds and those of other learners is one influential way to use the elements of inductive Bible study to create a lasting pedagogical impact. The study of characters frequently differs from digesting a single unit of Scripture, however, because by its very nature character study highlights an individual rather than other lessons the text might provide. And, of course, this also determines the unit or units selected for study.

Drs. Earle and Dorothy Bowen noticed in their work at Nairobi Evangelical Graduate School of Theology (NEGST) that the learning styles in east Africa differed significantly from those in the West. They developed the categories of "field independent" and "field sensitive," terms corresponding roughly to the more common educational nomenclature of left-mode (analytical) and right-mode (global, relational) cognitive strengths, and began testing students from around the world. The Bowens note that one of the strengths of the field-sensitive (global, relational) learner is meaningfully connecting with real-life human situations and stories. Further, when all characteristics of each cognitive strength are detailed in their research, they make the not-so-egalitarian point that field-independent (analytical) learners prefer to learn material when the curriculum is designed for their cognitive strengths but are still able to learn well when it is delivered in a field-sensitive fashion. Field-sensitive learners, on the other hand, can have great difficulty adjusting to the learning process when field-sensitive (global, relational) learning *isn't* utilized.

In short, the character study is human, relational, contains an illustrative dynamic and can impact all learning styles. This combination provides tremendous fodder for teaching the full spectrum of cognitive styles and is particularly beneficial for those given to right-mode/field-sensitive/global, relational strengths.

When proceeding, take the following steps as recommendations on how to maximize your time in the study of personalities in Scripture.

Gather Data and Record the Observations

Hans Finzel, in his excellent volume *Observe, Interpret, Apply*, suggests that in investigating a biblical personality the following facts should be considered: *name, birth, family background, early life/training, conversion, historical setting, role of geography, sin's role in life, spiritual life, major accomplishments, death and major lessons.* Since Ephesians was authored by Paul, let's utilize him and two other personalities mentioned in this chapter so far, David and Shamgar, to illustrate the use of character investigation. Paul's story is found, though not exclusively, in Acts. David's biography is included in I and II Samuel among other places. Shamgar appears in Judges 3:31.

Name - When putting together research notes on a personality, always consider the possible import of a given name. In the ancient Near East names frequently encompassed much more meaning than we accord them in our culture. They most often were bestowed as a quality for a person to live up to or in recognition of a person in the clan they were to replace upon that person's death. Shamgar is interesting at this point. It would take a study Bible or a good Bible dictionary for most of us to know that his wasn't a Hebrew name, for starters. And although the text doesn't tell us much about the circumstances, it must have been unusual for someone who probably wasn't an Israelite to answer the call of the Israelite God. Another interesting wrinkle—Shamgar is called *a son of Anath*. Anath was the sister of the pagan god, Baal. And God chooses to use him!

Are there lessons to be learned from the names David and Paul? Or from the name change in the New Testament from Saul to Paul? Do the individuals fulfill the destiny inherent in their names, or not? Why, why not? What are the full implications of all this data? These and the following items are essential topics to the character study.

Birth - where and when a person was born is helpful information for a timeline. Saul/Paul was born in Tarsus of Cilicia. An appropriate consideration such as this provides a good starting point for knowing Paul. David's hometown was Bethlehem, which, right questions asked, reveals much about this future king. Indeed, the "City of David" plays a huge role in the coming of the Messiah and provides a marker for future events both tragic and beautiful in the account of Jesus. *How does the place and time of birth impact the character? What is there about the person's place of birth or hometown that gives indication concerning the sort of individual that is described? What were the special circumstances of that place of origin in those particular years that may have influenced the person being studied? Do the location and the activities in that town/city lend any clues to possible character formation? Why is geography of this nature included in the biblical account?*

Family background - Paul's Roman citizenship, inherited from his father, would be a start for this investigation. David's family also provides material for study. We know that David was the youngest son of Jesse, whose quiver was already full of sons. Young David was humble, and he was overlooked and tended sheep. *How would this background affect later personality development? What can we learn about the individual from the way he was brought up? When do we see the family background become significant in influencing events in later life? How is this background beneficial or problematic for the person's life? When family background is included in the biblical account, why?*

Early life/training - Paul, as the thoroughgoing Jew he testified to be, must have lived a life of intense study and was a member of a devout family. On the other hand, David's shepherding and his subservient role in the lineup of brothers are instructive details as we examine some of the Psalms. And if Shamgar was really a non-Israelite, then what nationality was he? And what might his life typically have been like during his pre-judgeship era? *Who influenced these personalities, and what impact did these individuals carry with them because of that influence? What about the impact and training of early life that can be seen in later life? How were the individuals different from their peers in the life they led, the decisions they made, and the people they touched as a result of their previous lessons in life? Why was data on early life/training included?*

Conversion - Paul's conversion is a pivotal point in his life, no doubt about it. What influenced the pre-Damascus road experience? How was he different after it? At what point might David have experienced a birth, or rebirth, in God? *Who impacted the conversion experience? Who discipled the individual in life? Would the conversion experience become a marker to which the person would always refer? Why? How, exactly, did the conversion come about? How was the person different post-conversion? Why did the conversion/crisis point come in the way it did? Why was the conversion story included in the account?*

Historical setting - Again, if Shamgar was not an Israelite, how might he have perceived the history of the region? What was the history of Israel like during the time of David and how did it change in his lifetime? Add to Israel the influence of Rome when considering Paul at this point. And Israel, at the time of David, was in a unique point of its history—still getting used to having a king and all the implications of that scenario. *Who were the major players and what role did they have in the historical milieu of the character's time? What was unique about that place and time in human history? What was there about the historical setting that influenced the person being studied? What was the history of the geographic locale? What difference did that make on the personality? If the Bible is clear on some of this historical background, why did the writer of that portion of Scripture include that data?*

Role of geography - With reference to Paul, a brief study of a map of his missionary journeys provides deep insight into his vision, his undaunting drive, and his passion to spread the gospel in a day when few individuals traveled more than ten miles from their hometowns. David didn't stay in one place his entire life. What are the implications of his seemingly wayfaring meanderings? *The names and places of Scripture are frequently extensive in the life of the person studied. Why is this so? What critical role did geography play in the life of the person? Where did the person spend the most time? The least? Why? How did the geographical locale impact the timeline of the individual? Why is the geography of the individual's story even noteworthy?*

Sin's role in life - Of Shamgar we cannot be absolutely certain, but Paul and David both have sin stories worthy of contemplation. Paul's most apparent pre-Christian sin, assistance in the murder of Stephen, actually served as preparation for his imminent salvation. David's sins, his adultery/murder story, provide a major pivotal moment in his life. *Who were the major players in the "sin" stories? What vulnerabilities do these narratives describe? When does the character seem more vulnerable to sin? Less vulnerable? Any clues to be learned from where the sin happens or does not happen? There is always a "why" to sin. Why is it committed when it is? How does sin influence the story of this life? Why does the writer of the story include the details of sin?*

Spiritual life - David's and Paul's spiritual life stories are classics. David's can be traced through historical texts and the Psalms; Paul's can be substantially viewed through the book of Acts and in his epistles to various churches. *Who impacts the spiritual life of the person studied? What are the critical impacts of the renewed or deflated aspects of this spirituality? What difference does a person's spirituality make in an individual life? Does the spiritual life ebb and flow? Why? What happens when it is going well? When it is not? What makes for a deep spiritual life? For a shallow spiritual life? What are the characteristics of truly walking with God in this life? When, where and how does the spiritual life take an upturn? A downturn? Why are these details included in the account by the writer?*

Major accomplishments - Shamgar, David and Paul all boast major accomplishments; the stories of the latter two describe notable failures as well. *How were these noteworthy moments* *attained? Who was responsible? What impact did these accomplishments have on the individual? On the surrounding community/culture? What do we learn about the individual by particular feats? When in a person's life do things tend to get accomplished—spiritually? chronologically? intellectually? Is the "where" of these accomplishments important? How do the accomplishments come about? What can we discern by the author's inclusion of the accomplishments?*

Death - David's death is a powerful moment in Scripture, as he bids adieu to Solomon. We are left hanging with Paul and Shamgar although with Paul we might be able to surmise a few details. *Who played a role in these deaths? What impact did the death have upon family, followers, the culture, the nation? What can we learn from the death of the individual? Is the time of death critical? Why did the death have to occur? How did the death occur and what lessons can be derived from it? Why did the author include the details of death?*

Major lessons - As with most character studies in Scripture, major lessons from individual lives can be easily applied to modern believers. The list is short with Shamgar, perhaps. But with David and Paul the available data is extensive, as are the lessons. *After investigating the foregoing questions, what are the principles we can glean for our own personal growth and convey to our learning communities?*

Some find that a "timeline" is beneficial when putting together this data. It will help, but we have found that amassing the critical data and some answers to interpretive questions on a few pieces of paper is as beneficial. Indeed, if you write small and are adept at lists and charts a single page synopsis of even the most voluminous account of an individual in the Bible can give a helpful account of what the life was all about and how God tried to speak through that witness. The aim of the character study is obvious: to retrieve from biblical data a fair resume of a person's life and what can be learned from it. Frequently it is a different sort of exercise than picking out a unit of study and honing in on that text. While some character studies will be compact lessons from

Scripture, many will take the investigator across several pages, chapters or books. Aim for a tight, concise synopsis of one to two pages.

Character Studies and Structural Laws

Can structural laws work in character studies? Sometimes a single unit of Scripture makes the discovery of the operative structural laws tremendously beneficial. This would be true of Shamgar, for instance. Another interesting biblical character is Micaiah, a Hebrew prophet in the time of Ahab. One of the places you can find his story is in I Kings 22. Actually, it is the only story we know about Micaiah. But what a story! And yes, structural laws will help the reader discover much within that unit about this brave man.

But studying an individual in the Bible often involves multiple passages. When a single unit is not necessarily being considered, the use of structural laws can get tricky. In our estimation, however, the laws of composition are still applicable. For instance, if a timeline or chart can be constructed, structural laws are certainly relevant, even necessary:

- Was there a point of cruciality (a major turning point) in the life being studied?

- Were there contrasting/comparative elements in the personality or was there a contrasting/comparative character apparent in the text?

- Were there recurring features in the person being studied?

- What were the major problems to which there were obvious solutions?

- Does the person's life rise to a point of climax?

All these are absolutely critical questions that beg answers regardless of whether they are found in a single unit of study or multiple passages of Scripture. The use of structural laws as applied to the story of a life will provide interesting insights applicable for devotional or classroom purposes. Take the life of Jesus, for instance:

- Could it be argued that the temptation narrative in Matthew provided an interesting point of *cruciality* for Jesus?

- Did the author of the gospels include the Pharisees and Sadducees as *contrasting* elements in the story of the Lord?

- Are *recurring* elements like God's concern for the poor and a theme like the Kingdom of God fodder for continued investigation?

- What was the major problem Jesus faced?

- Does the resurrection comprise a climactic moment in the gospels?

These thoughts and inquiries only scratch the surface when applied to Jesus. And what of Paul? David? Other major characters of Scripture? The structural laws are tremendously enlightening when applied to the lives contained in the Word.

Character Studies and Extra-biblical Helps

Utilize other sources that fill in gaps that might exist in the biblical account. Bible dictionaries, Bible handbooks and atlases can be instructive in the correlation aspect of character study. A good Bible dictionary should give an abbreviated but thorough synopsis of the character's life and can also indicate other relevant data in Scripture. For example, a survey of Genesis is not adequate to complete a thorough character study of Abraham; the New Testament contains numerous references to the patriarch and some pretty substantial teaching as well. If the student is unaware of all the places in Scripture where Abraham is mentioned, a resource like a concordance will draw attention to additional biblical passages. A Bible handbook is a helpful reference tool which provides background on the Biblical world, commenting on historical, geographical and cultural subjects which shed light on the how and why of a character's behavior and thought process. Atlases provide not only maps, but also insight into the religious, military and economic aspects of Bible times.

Qualities to Emulate and to Avoid

Work diligently to identify qualities to emulate and characteristics to avoid. Since biblical characters are so human, there are both plenty of personal features to model and ample qualities to avoid. Most teachers consider these findings some of the best fodder for instruction.

But it is also some of the best material for meditation and devotion. Robert Mulholland, in *Shaped By the Word*, describes how he was once impressed in his devotional time by the character of Pharaoh. His study led him to perceive in Pharaoh the capacity to enslave God's people for selfish purposes in Egypt. Then, in what Mulholland suggests was a surprising moment even to him, he was impacted with the message that he was a slavemaster himself. Mulholland felt God impressing upon him that while possessing gifts and graces, talents and traits, he had enslaved them all for his own purposes and intentions instead of God's. That moment led to penetrating insight and necessary repentance.

Mulholland's experience illustrates one way that the Bible can have a powerful devotional effect. If the character study only impacts one's teaching audience, something has gone wrong in the process of Bible study. Indeed, one of Mulholland's central theses is that we are too caught up in an informational reading of Scripture and too little concerned with personal spiritual formation. To sacrifice the latter on the altar of the former spells spiritual tragedy for the growing Christian.

Make Character Studies Intimately Personal

Correlate the data with your life personally; also be cognizant of other biographies, both sacred and secular. Mulholland's incident in his study of Scripture and Pharaoh is a wonderful example of personal correlation. This is the sort of formational dynamic that ought to happen regularly with all manner of inductive Bible study but particularly with character study.

The three individuals already considered in this chapter, Shamgar, David and Paul, all possess characteristics that are worth pondering devotionally and communicating educationally. Shamgar had only an ox goad with which to kill hundreds of Philistines; David was only a shepherd and least of his brothers; Paul was an enemy of God's movement, struck blind on a road while heading to persecute the believers of Jesus. If we were to apply these seeming negatives seriously to our lives, we would have to ask: What things do we have through which God can work anyway? Introspectively, what weighs me down from being all God wants me to be? How did these men overcome the barriers to their victory? Do the stories contain clearly defined antidotes to failure? Potential questions, their application to the devotional life and illustrative opportunities for communication, are endless.

The basic outline of inductive study is relevant for character studies as well:

- Observe the data.

- Ask interpretive questions.

very nature presents the subject as "need to know" information. If the teacher is attuned to his students, it offers a tremendous bridge from student dilemmas to God's answers. Even so, perhaps point one in this chapter should be that learners' readiness correlates with what they need to know in order to effectively cope with the world around them. Teachers must be aware of this factor and topical studies should be selected with a need-to-know consideration.

Alfred North Whitehead, in the *Aims of Education*, described what he considered the rhythms of learning. One begins to learn a discipline with a romantic, playful approach before seeking to explore it with more intense, particular earnestness and finally, by generalizing the principles in life and communication.

Topical studies are a lot like that, beginning at the student's point of interest and moving to a deeper biblical perspective where necessary facts are considered and movement to principles of utility is offered. Whitehead made the case that the process never really ends, for learning is really the process of this cycle repeated over and again with deepening and more sophisticated levels of intelligence. The cycle, in other words, continues as it builds on previous information and enters new vistas of understanding.

This technique of the topical approach was demonstrated by Jesus in His ministry. One of the most dramatic examples is the story of the "Woman at the Well." Remember that as with so many of Jesus' teachings, the topics arose out of situations in which He found Himself amidst His everyday journeys. While the Bible scholar will be able to draw from situations, build a lesson on those situations in the study and carry the lesson into the classroom, Jesus frequently performed His rapid fire lesson delivery on the spot. One day the gospel account of John says that He had to go through Samaria and came upon a town called Sychar. Jesus sat down by the well, and the situation He found

Himself in gave rise to a great topical lesson. You can find it in John 4:4-30, 39-42.

The Topic: *Living water*

The Romance:
- The account opens as Jesus inquires about a drink from a Samaritan woman. The account suggests this is quite out of the ordinary, since Jews don't associate with Samaritans.
- Jesus challenges her to consider living water.
- She becomes more interested.
- And who is He to be talking about living water?

The Particularization of Jesus:
- The water I give will satisfy your thirst forever.
- The water I give wells up to eternal life.

The Generalization (Internalization) of the Woman and Friends:
- The woman goes back to her town and invites the people to come and discover the man who could be the Christ.
- Many Samaritans came to believe in Him because of the woman's testimony.
- Jesus stays with them; many more become believers.
- Jesus is proclaimed the "Savior of the World."

As with the woman at the well, topical studies born from situations that challenge students in the contemporary age are an extremely effective means of transmitting truth. These studies should pique interest, lead learners to more intricate nuances of the topic and help them to internalize the truths for themselves. There may be times when the educator transmits a lesson situationally and "on-the-spot," not unlike many of Jesus' lessons. Much of the time, however, topics arrived at situationally can be studied further for communication in a classroom at a later time.

With the latter in mind, the following are some keys to consider when seeking to employ this most effective method of Bible study for instruction.

The Topical Study As Unit Study

We have already made the case that a single topical study will frequently require research scattered across many pages of Scripture. Nevertheless, sometimes all that is required for a topical Bible study is a unit of Scripture that teaches about the subject of choice. The editors of the popular group-study *Serendipity Bible* suggest many possible topics in its opening pages. If you are working through some problems in your life, you might want to go to Genesis 11:1-9 and the story of the tower of Babel (a study in self-worth), or to the famous episode about Balaam's ass in Numbers 22:21-35 (procrastination). If you're tempted to abandon a task, how about the Jonah narrative (Jonah 1)? Rejection? Try the nation of Israel turning from Samuel and his sons and demanding a king instead (1 Samuel 8). The point is that one can cover a "topic" pretty significantly with a single unit of Scripture. Therefore, all that is really necessary for a good topical study is an interesting unit of Scripture well-observed, responsibly interpreted, thoroughly correlated and diligently applied. To complete this kind of study is to apply the steps of inductive Bible study to the unit most applicable to the topic at hand.

But for the alternative method of examining a series of Scripture passages in several areas of the Bible, here are some suggestions on how to proceed.

Amassing the Tools

Topical Bible studies are frequently best undertaken with the following tools: imagination, a concordance and a Bible with cross-references. Let's examine each of these tools in light of the elements essential for a topical study that will come alive for the teacher-in-study and the audience which receives it:

a. Your imagination. There is no end to the number of topics that can be examined, and your first source should be Scripture itself. In Ephesians, numerous life-issues can be explored in and beyond the epistle itself. One example is God's roadmap for our lives. Almost everybody wants to know God's plan for their lives. In the first part of the opening chapter, Ephesians tackles that issue in the form of predestination. How about the topic of spiritual sight or God's 20/20 vision as found in the second half of the same chapter? Consider the topic of racial reconciliation, a prominent theme of chapters two and three. Or what makes for a winning team (chapter four)? What about the family that imitates God (chapter five)? And the cosmic fight (chapter six)? These topics are clearly present, ready to be coordinated with other verses in the Bible to provide a full topical resumé of matters that are on the minds of both God and His people.

One need not start with the Bible when imagining subjects to be covered in Scripture. Jesus didn't limit Himself like that, nor did Paul. Their environment mattered, as did the issues of the day. Magazines, newspapers, books, life experiences, history, crises, relationships, moral issues, attitudes and social concerns all provide excellent resources for finding a topic that will resonate with your learning community or that simply meets a need.

A youth pastor we know reads *Seventeen* magazine in order to understand what the adolescent females in his group are exposed to and to discover how it is shaping their thinking. While some pastors might never want to let their eyes fall upon a *Cosmopolitan* magazine, it and magazines like *Ebony*, *Essence* and *Gentleman's Quarterly* can provide great idea starters for communicating truth to those living in the secular world. Consider topics like "Most Admired People" and "Best Dressed" and "Get in Shape for the Summer" and "Six Ways to be a Better Lover." Does the Bible have anything to say on these subjects? Definitely! How about a series on "My Most Admired Biblical Woman"? Or, "The Best Dressed Men" that deals with men in

Scripture who adorned their lives with the holiness of God. Or, a lesson on how to get in shape for the summer that addresses spiritual fitness. And that topic about better loving? The Bible deals significantly with God's extraordinary loving-kindness for His people and how that love ought to impact us. If a Christian educator wants to address a more erotic kind of affection, the Song of Solomon provides plenty of material for study.

Some might consider these topics a little too frivolous or, at the least, based upon frothy idea-starters. Just remember that an idea in embryonic form can definitely flower into something far more substantial with further consideration and study.

There are other sources, of course. Recently in a Sunday school class in Mississippi the teacher started off by asking everyone what they thought of the recent situation in a nearby high school. A teenage boy killed two and injured seven others in a shooting spree. The class, as had the community as a whole, expressed outrage. At that point, the teacher launched into a study of Jesus' words on murder in the Sermon on the Mount. These verses lead right into strong denunciations of anger, name-calling and reconciliation. Because the facilitator handled the situation with aplomb, students who had vented their anger about the murder became duly humbled at the words of Jesus. The entire class learned a valuable lesson. Suffice it to say that the local or national newspaper provides a great resource for topics that are on the minds of the audience.

Another resource for topical ideas is radio and television: news, talk shows, sports and entertainment. Years ago, a popular sitcom's theme song suggested that it was great to go to a place where everybody knew your name, where they were always glad you came and where the problems are all the same. That line in the theme song has provided a good starting point for many a discussion contemplating Christian community. Interestingly enough, the same show's cast ended up obviously drunk on a talk show after the final episode aired, which proved the disparity between reality and acting a part. That opened up an entirely different kind of Sunday school lesson out of Matthew 23 on the Greek word *hypokrisis*, from which the word "hypocrite" is derived. This particular word in the ancient language originally described actors who put masks over their faces in order to hide their real identities.

The various life situations we commonly experience provide plenty of opportunities to teach topically. Environmental disasters, ill health, deaths, divorce, bankruptcies, and political corruption comprise some of life's enduring, if lamentable, situations with which to search Scripture. Family life, friendships, future opportunities, meaningful work and recreation are a few more upbeat issues that could be addressed. Imagination in the Christian educator and an open eye to possibilities in our various endeavors are some of God's best tools for the study of the Bible.

Choose a topic and then locate passages in Scripture where it might be addressed. To do this, your own work in the Bible will be helpful, and memory will serve as an aid, but there are tools which will also assist in this endeavor.

b. Concordance. A concordance is simply an alphabetical list of words in the Bible with references to passages where they occur. To find a topic in Scripture, all relevant words should be looked up and parallel passages investigated. Depending upon the subject and concomitant words, this can be a relatively brief or an incredibly lengthy process. The student of Scripture must make the decision to be either exhaustive or selective in the passages which give the best resumé of what the Bible has to say on the subject.

For example, let's say that the murder of someone in your community is your idea-starter. In the foregoing illustration of something similar in Mississippi, the passage from Matthew 5:1-11 was cited. But obviously that is not the only place in

Scripture where murder is discussed. In fact, there are some eighty references in the New International Version concordance for murder, murdered, murderer, murderers, murdering, murderous and murders. A survey of these terms and their various uses provides quite a study to address a community tragedy.

But what if we were to do a study on "getting the Body of Christ in shape for the summer"? Various terms could be researched, but "Body of Christ" should obviously be checked, as should "spiritual"; and, once the study is underway, other terms worth investigating might come to mind or emerge from the text such as: fellowship, prayer, service, worship, study, compassion, etc.

c. Bible with cross-references. Once relevant passages are identified, some Bibles contain excellent cross-references to additional, related verses. Sometimes the destination to which these references lead may be profitable; in other instances they may end up being further off the subject than the student of the Bible deems helpful for the particular study at hand. Topical Bibles such as *Nave's Topical Bible* and *Thompson's Chain Reference Bible*, can help greatly in this regard. These resources can be exhaustive, but again, depending on the subject, the educator may not have time for "exhaustive." So, choose your most helpful sources wisely.

Observation: Critical Key to Topical Study

The principles in chapter three of this volume should be followed in the study of a topic. *The reportorial questions (Who, What, When, Where, How and Why) should be utilized and the structural laws sought* if the relevant passage is of significant size. Study thoroughly the main passages of teaching on the subject. If, for instance, we considered every possible avenue of investigation for "getting the Body of Christ in shape," the study might last several days, or weeks, or months. Since time is frequently of the essence, the researcher should identify major teachings and the most cogent passages. This task takes a discerning eye. But discernment is the key to good observation.

Keep a notepad handy when consolidating your findings. Topical studies require a basic puzzle placement skill: that is, taking the various pieces of the study and trying to fit them all together into a coherent whole. During the observation phase of topical study take plenty of well-organized notes with the goal of assembling these notes into a few major points. Remember, if most of these main points can be found in a single or a few units of Scripture, begin focusing on these passages. Then use the other verses to buttress your focus on these primary biblical portions.

Interpret and Correlate

As chapter four indicates, good interpretation is the art of asking more questions and then seeking the answers either in the Bible or in other important pieces of extra-biblical literature. *Part of the interpretation process in topical study is correlation—asking yourself what other Scriptures and life experiences are relevant.*

- Are there other passages relating to this topic?

- Are other books written on this theme?

- Does the data relate to anything in the local media or in your own life or group experience?

Correlation is extremely important to inductive Bible study because illustration of various points is what really makes the study come alive when presented to a class of students. Books tend to be very helpful at this juncture because by their very nature they are written by topic. A card catalog or a trip through a local bookstore can provide numerous ideas.

Because topics should be chosen in part due to their resonance with the particular set of students, correlation should be considered with the audience's life experiences in mind. Interviews and informal conversations provide potent illustrative material, although permission should be received before divulging stories.

Consider Doctrine for Topics

There are numerous areas to explore theologically. Some of the major fields include:

- theism, the doctrine of an encountering, personal God

- anthropology, the doctrine of man

- hamartiology, the study of sin

- soteriology, the study of salvation

- revelation and inspiration, the study of the Word of God

- Christology, the study of the incarnation of God

- the Trinity, the study of the three-person Godhead

- pneumatology, the study of the Holy Spirit

- ecclesiology, the study of the church

- missiology, the study of God's redemptive mission and man's responsibility in that divine purpose

- social involvement, the study of the compassionate responsibility of the people of God

- ethics, the study of God's standards for man

- angelology and demonology, the study of intelligent nonhuman creatures

- eschatology, the study of last things in the redemptive plan of God

This list constitutes only the main categories of theological inquiry but these ought to serve as interest generators when considering the rich fields of doctrinal study in the Word. Sub-categories exist and tend to proliferate the deeper into a subject one chooses to go.

The challenge when the topic is a doctrine is to find biblical teachings on the subject matter you have chosen. This can happen in at least a couple of different ways. In the course of studying Ephesians, for instance, the existence of some profound theology becomes obvious. While it would be a limited study (and all theological inquiries are, in fact, limited) one could ask some of the most basic questions of the text and arise from that unit with a significant, if not entire, theology of God, or perhaps Christ, or man or sin and salvation or—and the blank can be filled with other topics addressed by Paul in his letter. For instance, were Christology the field of theological exploration, one would find every single chapter of Ephesians replete with remarkable insight. While inexhaustive, Ephesians alone contains ample lessons on the Person of Christ.

To include other portions of Scripture, as they surely should be for a fuller picture of the doctrine under investigation, utilize a concordance and search for key and related words. Following are some key word examples (by no means exhaustive) for hamartiology and revelation:

- hamartiology: evil, devil, offense, profane, Satan, sin, transgression, wicked

- revelation and inspiration: authority, commands, decrees, inspiration, revelation, statutes, Word

The concordance easily leads to strategic verses that can shed great light on the theology of sin and revelation, or harmatiology, using these words as preliminary investigative clues.

The key in topical and doctrinal investigation is to focus on significant passages. Clearly, there will be numerous passages relating to each doctrinal issue. The Bible student must therefore narrow the focus and select important sections upon which to concentrate study. The student will want to a) perform word studies and b) be cognizant of the structural laws in the context in which the words appear. This step in the process of theological inquiry is not unlike that covered in the following chapter on word study.

For example, if you are studying the theology of Christ, or Christology, and launching the study from the epistle to the Ephesians, a number of words would merit further investigation: Christ, Jesus, Lord, grace, love, redemption, love, forgiveness, blood, head, glory, salvation, power, right hand, church, body. Now, those words were chosen from the first chapter and do not encompass all critical terms. But to explore interlocking terms and units to present the person of Jesus in Scripture is a sure invitation to expand one's working knowledge of the Bible and Christ, and to identify additional doctrinal topics for further observation and analysis.

Another matter is significant, though, as one selects those passages which will become the foundation of the subject at hand. The student must keep the whole picture in mind and select passages which reflect the progressive revelation of a particular doctrine. Watch to see how the doctrine deepens as it moves from first mention to continued and final exposure: through the books of Law, history, prophets, poetry, gospels, early church history, epistles and apocalyptic literature. The Bible covers the span of thousands of years; truth never changes but the way that God communicates to man and builds on previous lessons is a profound study.

One final word concerning doctrinal study: Correlation is critical. As we have already written an entire chapter on correlation, let us focus for a moment on the work of other scholars. An intellectual giant of the twentieth century, C.S. Lewis, wrote in *Mere Christianity* that while theology is not the real thing—not, in other words, an experience with God—it is a lot like a map based on the experiences of thousands of people who have walked on the land and sea and have written down their findings to show us the way. In the same way, theology is a map, based on the experiences of thousands of people. Correlation with great experiencers of the faith is invaluable. We have much to learn from Augustine, Aquinas, Luther, Calvin, Wesley and others. To check theological accuracy, read not only these scholars but also contemporary theologians who take the Bible seriously and who build on these "greats." The correlative process that yields itself to the wisdom of brilliant theologians in the orthodox tradition is an essential aspect of the doctrinal study.

Topical and doctrinal studies, when done correctly, require discipline, integrity and tenacity. In actuality, they are much like word study, but more comprehensive. The goal is to give an accurate representation of what God through Scripture has to say about a subject or doctrinal emphasis. This is certainly a tall order; but for the Bible scholar, an essential one.

CHAPTER 10

Word Study

The word study is one of the most enjoyable forays into Bible study. The insights gleaned are frequently enlightening and can aid enormously in understanding biblical passages both large and small. Here are a few insights from this, the smallest unit of inductive Bible study:

- The Greek word for "meek" doesn't mean "wimp," but power under control. It referred in earlier biblical days to the domestication of wild animals (specifically, horses).

- The Hebrew *yada* (know) was first used with a sexual connotation (Adam *knew* Eve) and really meant "to experience" or "to encounter." Only later did it come to describe the non-sexual, but intimate, relationship between God and man.

- The cognate of the Hebrew word for salvation (*yash*) actually means "to make broad," "to make roomy."

- The Old Testament word for holy—*qadosh*—was used first in Exodus 3 in reference to the ground on which

Moses was standing—an important first lesson for Moses that wherever the presence of God is, that place is holy.

- The etymology of one of the Greek words for teach—*didasko*—leads some scholars to believe that it means, in its most basic form, *"to extend the hand to, repeatedly."* Apparently "teach" was a relational term.

From the pages of Scripture come fascinating insights that lead to vital conceptual frameworks built piece by piece, insight by insight, and word by word.

Think of it: books are made up of sections, sections of chapters, chapters of sentences, sentences of phrases and phrases of words. Know words and you will understand phrases. Become an expert at phrases and you can become an authority at sentences. Master sentences and you will figure out paragraphs. Comprehend paragraphs and then become adept at sections. Interpret sections with aptitude and you will read books—and in our case, the Book—deeply and well.

Words are the fundamental building blocks of the whole, and to grasp the nuances of a particular word is to commence on a wonderful journey of learning. This is why, of course, the word study is so critical to inductive Bible study. To observe-interpret-correlate-apply at this level of literature is to get the entirely opposite, but equally important, worm's eye view—as opposed to the bird's eye view! Seeing the parts are every bit as necessary as seeing the whole, and equally challenging.

Word study should normally take place as a very specific point of interest and inquiry in the midst of unit, topical, character or doctrinal study. In the course of the "bird's eye" overview, the Bible student may notice a term that is crucial, or interesting or confusing, and recognize it as worthy of further study. To pursue that interest or intellectual challenge is what word study is all about. Done well, it can significantly enliven the more generalized approach and add a perspective that is life-changing, for there is power in even a single word of Scripture properly, appropriately and thoroughly probed.

The research of Drs. Earle and Dorothy Bowen was noted in chapter eight. Their categories of "field independent" and "field sensitive," correspond with right and left-brained strengths in popular research parlance. Character study, as has been noted, is most appropriate for the field-sensitive (right-mode, global, relational) learner because of its human and personal approach. Word study plays to the strength of the analytical (field-independent) learner, however, because successful study of a term is facilitated by linguistic aptitude and the ability to notice and appreciate differences and details. Regardless of which conceptual strength is more suited for word study, this technique is vital for everyone who wants to strengthen the mind for God. Indeed, suggest the Bowens, each learning strength needs the other—the global, relational learner can be sharpened by the analytical, precise and detailed mode of perception. On the other hand, if the field-independent learner is never challenged by the field-sensitive approach, something precious and even necessary has been lost for that learner. Strengths are to be noted and taken advantage of, but the entire intellect must be addressed if maximum cognitive impact is to be attained.

Word study—the intense attention afforded a single word—has many benefits, but it can be especially beneficial in the study of doctrine. Theology has been described as the systematic presentation of what God thinks about a subject. Word study is critical as there are always key terms that must be mastered before a thorough grasp of theological truth can be attained. Understanding of essential terminology can add greatly to a growing mastery of theological thinking.

Word studies are enjoyable, challenging and full of eye-opening opportunities for intellectual expansion. Earnest study of these building blocks of the Bible yields rewarding insights and will deepen the perspective of learners and educators in the pursuit of scriptural knowledge.

Dabbling in Greek and Hebrew

Get a concordance and learn a little bit about ancient biblical languages. Several courses in seminary language studies aren't necessary, although the authors concede having taken a few. The study of ancient languages at a rudimentary level, while it sounds daunting to those who read only from the English text, is remarkably easy given a few of the right books and a little work. The Bible has been translated from mostly Hebrew (Old Testament) and Greek (New Testament) and finding exact English equivalents for every Hebrew or Greek word is not always possible. Using an exhaustive concordance, therefore, can be very helpful when conducting word studies. Here is an example why: The word for "teach" in Exodus 4:12 is different than the word for "teach" in Exodus 18:20. When doing a word study on "teach" in Exodus 4:12 it is important to compare other uses of the same Hebrew word.

An exhaustive concordance, which has numbers keyed to definitions in the back of the concordance, makes these differences plain. It is simply a matter of knowing the difference between numbers, not the difference between Hebrew letters. In fact, *Strong's Exhaustive Concordance of the Bible* gives seven different words used for "teach" in the Hebrew and seven in the Greek— and all have rich meanings. Consider, for instance, the Hebrew words:

- "Alaph" — to become familiar with, to accustom oneself, to befriend

- "Bin" — to distinguish, to separate, to discern, to see distinctions, to perceive

- "Yada" — to know, to acquaint, encounter, experience
- "Yarah" — to direct, cast, throw, shoot, to point the way
- "Zahar" — to enlighten, to warn, to caution, to admonish, to shine
- "Lamad" — to goad, to instruct diligently
- "Shanan" — to inculcate, to sharpen, to prick, to teach diligently

And some of the Greek words for "teach":

- "Didasko" — to teach, to accept, to extend the hand to
- "Didaktikos" — apt to teach
- "Heterodidaskaleo" — to instruct differently
- "Katecheo" — to sound from above with emphasis on becoming orally informed and questioned
- "Katagello" — to proclaim, to declare, to preach
- "Matheteo" — to make a disciple of
- "Rhipizo" — to fan, to agitate

Some reportorial questions that might accompany these words:

- *Who* uses them?
- *About whom* are they used (i.e., which are used of Jesus, of Paul, of the disciples)?

- *What* are the different nuances of meaning when they are utilized?

- *When* is each term used?

- In *what* circumstances is one term used over another?

- *Why* use one term over another?

- *Why* is one used more than any other? Less?

- *How* could a scriptural lesson be differently impacted with the use of another teaching word?

The Hebrew and Greek review of "teach"—which seems to be a simple term in English—reveals nuances behind this "single" word that span fourteen different terms in two languages. This sort of discovery will lend vital insight. By checking the meaning in the back of the concordance and by comparing and contrasting these definitions, even a student with no working knowledge of the original languages can be led to meaningful biblical truth. But, in the interest of the observation techniques already explained in this volume, the greatest benefit of the concordance accrues as students compare and contrast for themselves various nuances of meaning.

Perspective is Key to Word Study

When studying a key word, first get a *perspective* on its use in the verse where it originally occurs (*observation*). Just knowing a dictionary or concordance definition won't fill you in on all that can or should be known about a word. Important beginning questions:

- *Why* is the word used this way?

- *Why* did the author use this word instead of another?

- *What* is the context within which the word is found?

- If no other usage could be located, *what* might you suggest the word used there and then means?

Then, move on to other verses which contain the same term. Always note the context. Sometimes context reveals more about the word than does the formal definition itself. After thoroughly examining the word in its context, with the help of a key word concordance find other places where that word is found. Study the term in various contexts. Variations include: examining the word within a single book and in other books/epistles by the same author and comparing the different uses in the Old versus New Testaments.

In Ephesians, one recurring term is "grace." The concordance dictionary defines grace (*charis*) as the divine influence on the heart and its reflection in the life. It occurs eleven times in Ephesians and 127 times in the New Testament. In the Pauline epistles alone, it appears 89 times.

After examining "grace" in the epistle to the Ephesians, this is what an observer might be able to presume:

- **Grace** and peace ride in tandem and are given to the Ephesians by the Godhead (1:2).

- **Grace** is so good it is to be lauded, and came to the Ephesians freely by a loving One (1:6).

- In **grace** there is lavish "wealth"—redemption of sins through His blood, forgiveness of sins (1:7-8).

- **Grace** made the Ephesians alive and has saved them even though they were formerly sinners, spiritually dead, with an evil spirit at work in them, and even though they previously were busy gratifying sinful cravings (2:1-5).

- These riches are not only lavish but incomparable! They were expressed to us in Jesus. The Ephesians were not saved by themselves, not by works, but by God's **grace** through faith (2:7-9).

- Paul was not the source of that **grace**, but it was given him through the power of God that Gentiles might know the lavish and incomparable riches that had, up to that time, been kept a mystery (2:7-9).

- This **grace** has been given to all the Ephesians, in a variety of ways, that God's people might serve to build the body of Christ and assist in reaching unity, knowledge and maturity—the fullness of Christ.

Bit by bit, piece by piece, the parts of the grace puzzle come together and reveal a powerful lesson in the phenomenal, lavish love and mercy of God. A relatively simple three chapter investigation results in a list that is now waiting for the further natural inquiries of the *Who/What/When/Where/How/Why* nature.

Also, note what has just happened through this word study: a rich beginning to an understanding of the theology of grace, of redemption, indeed, of Christ. This is what we mean when we suggest that a single word study can move the investigator far down the road to substantial doctrinal understanding.

Interpret and Draw Conclusions

Next, *formulate conclusions about how the word is used* in various contexts and the different applications of the term *(interpretation)*. From the Ephesians investigation the following might be supposed:

> ***Grace*** *is related to peace because only grace can bring harmony with God. It is a free gift that the Ephesians didn't deserve, given by One who loved them and wanted to bless them by forgiving their wickedness and saving them from its effects. In order for grace to have this effect, the Ephesians had to put their faith in God. Jesus is the distributor of God's grace, although He chose also to use Paul and the Ephesians through their gifts. These grace-filled gifts were to be used to serve Christ and build His body.*

That is not all that Paul teaches about grace. Nor is it all the New or Old Testaments teach. Truth be known, it is not all that Ephesians teaches. But it is a good start, made possible through word study.

Check Secondary Sources

Check results with secondary sources (correlate). Having investigated grace according to Paul, might some other resources prove beneficial? While it should never be the first stop in word study, we have already noted that correlation is critical and surveying what other scholars have learned about the subject of grace will undoubtedly inform one's perspective.

- The *NIV Study Bible* describes grace, from Paul's perspective as God's kindness, and as unmerited favor and forgiving love. In the third chapter, the *NIVSB* says that grace becomes a special gift that brings with it responsibility for divine service.

- William Barclay in *The Daily Bible Study Series* says that man can make atonement for a broken law, but not for a broken heart, and that sin is not so much broken law as it is the breaking of the heart of God. Only God's grace accepted by man is able to heal that broken relationship.

- In *Wesley's Notes on the New Testament,* John Wesley suggests that the Pauline concept was of grace given irrespective of human worthiness; faith, with emptied hand, receives it.

- *The Theological Dictionary of the New Testament* offers unique insight into the secular Greek usage of *charis*. Aeschylus used it to denote the favor of the gods. In Hellenism, *charis* was a term to show the favor of a ruler. Also in Hellenism grace came from above, appeared in the divine man, and expressed itself magically. *Charis* as the divine favor revealed in Christ was a distinctively Pauline concept.

- *The Dictionary of New Testament Theology* says that words developed from the Greek root *char* signify things that produce well-being. *Charis* is used 155 times, one hundred of which occur in the Pauline letters. It is obviously central to Paul's thought, which is why he places it at the beginning and end of his letters. It is more than just a trite greeting and salutation: it really does bracket his view of the faith.

This brief survey of resources gives an idea of how other scholars' works might prove beneficial to a fuller understanding of a selected word. Anthologies of favorite authors such as Oswald Chambers, E. Stanley Jones, A.W. Tozer and C.S. Lewis also prove useful.

Dictionaries are most helpful tools in Bible study, particularly those that give the etymology of words. "Educate" comes from the Latin *ex* (out) + *ducere* (to lead). The word means to develop the knowledge, skill or character. From the Latin, it is leading a learner from one place to another; from one state of being/doing to a better condition. It doesn't take much imagination to find powerful scriptural examples of the Godhead involved in *educating* long before the incarnation of Jesus. Not the least of these occasions was the exodus (from the Greek *ex*/out + *hodos*/the way—"the way out") where the Educator led the people of Israel out of bondage and servitude to a pagan king, into the Promised Land. To be fair, many scholars eschew considering etymologies noting that a word's origins (especially if the word is from the Latin) hardly gives an accurate idea of how it was used in a biblical account. This is often true, which is why etymological considerations should only make up as a small part of a larger whole. But we find that etymologies are helpful when they buttress a sound point already obvious in word comparisons and contrasts found within the Bible itself. Also they serve as helpful addendums to accurate word study scholarship.

In any case, a simple English dictionary can be of great assistance. One hint: keep one handy at all times to look up words like "grace." Grace comes, by the way, from the Latin *gratus* meaning "pleasing." The first definition listed is beauty or charm of form, movement or expression. That correlates nicely, of course, with the rest of the study in Paul's teaching to the Ephesians regarding *charis*. Here is a case when the correlation can be utilized for helpful communication purposes and we have no problem, therefore, using such an insight. It is notable how many times a simple dictionary can help when studying the Bible. As an earlier paragraph in this book indicated, Dr. Wilbert White dreamed of the day when his students could take a Bible and a dictionary and be ready to deliver scriptural truth no matter their circumstances.

One other tip when tracing words through Scripture: Note the progression of the word. "Holy" (*qadosh*) is a good example of a word that gains depth of meaning each step of the way through Scripture. It is found some eight times in Paul's letter to the Ephesians and while these are all very insightful a more thorough investigation into the Hebraic development also is beneficial. It is interesting to observe the word, and the doctrine of holiness that grows up around it, through the books of Law, history, prophets, poetry, gospels, early church history, epistles and apocalyptic literature.

The Bible covers a span of thousands of years. The way God communicates to people, and people with each other, is bound to change over time. In the *Beacon Dictionary of Theology*, Old Testament and Semitic language scholar Dennis Kinlaw considers the development of the word "holy." It was first used by the Canaanites to differentiate the religious from the irreligious, but the religious at that time and in that place included temple prostitutes and homosexual priests. So when language is used to describe the sacred in Scripture, God, says Kinlaw, had to fill that language with new meaning. In Exodus 3:5 the process begins. The ground on which Moses stands is holy. Why? Because God is there. From that point on in Scripture, "holy" refers only to Jehovah and the things associated with Him, whether that be ground, assemblies, days, oils, foods, clothing or persons.

When New Testament communication commenced there were five Greek words meaning holy from which the biblical authors could choose. With rare exception, the New Testament authors selected *hagios*, the term least used in classical Greek. The unique character of God, according to Kinlaw, demanded a relatively unique approach. This is also the same word that describes God in the person of the Holy Spirit.

The word "holy," therefore, has been used variously and across many languages; from Canaanite worship to Sinai dirt to the third person of the Trinity. There is a progression of terminology, but more than that, evidence of a growing relationship between God and man and a growing revelation of who God is.

Produce a Resumé of Findings

A resumé, as mentioned earlier in this volume, is a summary or a distillation. The challenge in word study is creating and presenting an accurate resumé of findings, without overemphasizing one component of God's truth at the expense of another. To fail here is to create a springboard for error, even heresy.

A summary of Ephesians should note that the epistle does not deal primarily with the theology of "holiness." But there is a "holy" message here, and to miss that is to bypass an important point. If an accurate picture of Ephesians is to be presented, how significant a place should the Pauline concept of "holy" assume? That, of course, is up to the communicator. But one would be wrong to overemphasize the use of that word at the expense of "grace" or the essential contrasts of the epistle, or the structural law of comparative causation. An objective look at the words and the resulting theology as filtered through the observation-interpretation-correlation-application cycle will allow the student to grant appropriate weight to the various components of the study. When the study of a unit is complete, essential lessons of that unit should be placed on paper for review. If the study is thorough, a word study (or several) will be added to that summary.

Sometimes, of course, an entire word study can stand on its own merit. That study will need to reflect a fair analysis of the various uses found and each nuance given its appropriate due. This is a somewhat subjective process. However, with time and practice it will lead the learner to remarkable reservoirs of insight.

What is interesting about all the parts of an epistle study or even a stand-alone word study is the many parts that come together to make an intriguing whole. We have found that the process by which these parts congeal into an accurate biblical picture is reminiscent of a kaleidoscope. The tube of a kaleidoscope holds a variety of multi-sized and colored crystals. The images of the crystals bounce off a V-shaped reflector, which extends through the center of the tube, creating a circular image for the viewer. By rotating the end of the kaleidoscope, one can shift the colorful crystals into new configurations. Each detailed word study that budding scholars complete can be compared to the addition of a new crystal in their kaleidoscope, enriching the colors, shapes and patterns of their perspective on biblical truth.

The Kaleidoscope

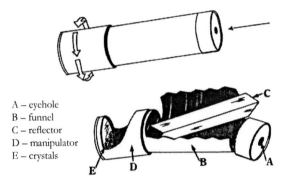

A – eyehole
B – funnel
C – reflector
D – manipulator
E – crystals

One more thing about the kaleidoscope: it works best when held up to the light. And word study, as with all inductive Bible study, is most fruitful when the final product is held up to the light of God.

CHAPTER 11

Teaching What Has Been Learned

We have seen it over and over again. People learn the various steps and implementations of inductive Bible study. Having applied their new-found methodology to their Bibles in pursuit of truth, they can hardly wait for the next opportunity to present their discovered knowledge to others.

Sometimes the sheer zeal of their newfound enthusiasm for the Word is enough to carry them through to successful communication. Often, however, their insights fall to the wayside because they forgot to employ a few techniques that could have kept their audience from a midday nap.

Inductive Bible study for most passionate Christians has not fulfilled its purpose until truth found is truth taught and until truth on the listening audience's part is received and applied. Learning for the sake of one's own personal growth is most certainly worthwhile. But the greater goal is to deliver biblical insights and their life implications to an audience willing to listen. This is why inductive study is an absolute must in our lives. So, effective communication is a matter worth considering in a volume on Bible study.

This chapter will concentrate on this necessary dynamic of communication. Once the observation-interpretation-correlation-application cycle is completed and a unit, character, topic/doctrine and/or word has been studied and appropriately understood, then it is time to tell others about one's findings. This chapter shows the reader how to take the combined lessons from each phase of inductive study and create a teaching module that will impress biblical principles upon students' minds, hearts and hands.

As explained by Asbury Theological Seminary professor, Ralph Lewis, the bridge between solid data and effective presentation involves moving from the unknown, the abstract and the universal to the known, the concrete and the personal. One example is Jesus' use of the parable. That English word for parable derives from the Greek: *para-* (beside) + *ballein* (to throw). Jesus' stories were just that—concrete and provocative illustrations *thrown beside* an as yet unknown Kingdom truth to make it understandable. More than a mere teaching technique, however, that actually describes the incarnation of Jesus: throwing a tent of flesh alongside humankind and demonstrating the reality of God in a known, concrete and personal way.

If we were to examine one passage of Scripture to illustrate how Jesus moved his students from the unknown to the known, the Sermon on the Mount in Matthew would be a good starting point. Ralph Lewis analyzed the Sermon and was struck by the following findings:

- 1/7th of the sermon involved images, pictures, examples and illustrations (wolves, sheep, fruit, light, rock, sand, storm, build, etc.)

- comparisons comprised 1/16th

- 1/6th contained verbs relating to energy/action

- 65% of the sermon was delivered in the present tense for relevance and realism

- 30% dealt with the future tense and

- 5% was past tense

Jesus' presentation in Matthew 5, 6 and 7 also contained variety. He accomplished this by describing forty-two different aspects of happiness and asking nineteen questions. According to Lewis, this gives the lesson an overall feel of dialogue and involvement on the part of the learner.

Since Jesus was a master teacher, why don't we just use His material verbatim? This might work, and frequently does. But if Jesus were incarnate in a 21st century, technological society, He most likely wouldn't be using illustrations concerning wolves, sheep, sand, Samaritans, fig trees and wineskins. So what would He use?

Robert Sheldon once wrote a book entitled *In His Steps* which posed the question, *What would Jesus do?* For the educator, one thing is certain: He wouldn't take a life-changing message and bore people with it. He would, and did, make biblical principles come alive. And yet David Preus, bishop emeritus of the former American Lutheran Church, remarked that after thirty-nine years of ministry he was forced to admit that the greatest public sin of those in the ministry was that we are boring.

How can we change that?

Grace, Going Before

Heretofore in this volume we have suggested that prayer is an essential precursor to actually studying God's Word, a call to God for illumination. In the presentation phase, however, prayer takes on a bit different purpose. The theological concept known as *prevenient grace* refers to God's activity that "goes before" conversion. When preparing material for presentation, we would do well to ask God to "go before" our efforts at teaching by preparing the heart of each individual listener to receive His message.

Prevenient grace as a concept is usually used in conjunction with salvation. That is, God, by grace, prepares a person for reception of the salvation message. But this grace is also available as we pray for God to prepare others to hear His Word out of Ephesians and respond appropriately to the biblical directive it contains. We ask the Lord to infill the small group dynamic, blending hearts to create an advantageous learning environment. We pray that the message being prepared in the study and the accompanying educational activities will have optimum influence. If we really believe in a God who is active in our places of service, then we must also believe in a God who will gladly respond when we ask Him to work on behalf of the Kingdom and the part our biblical presentation plays in it. The educator benefits from praying daily for this sort of "prevenient grace" and over time will notice the difference it makes in the classroom.

Keep Files and Resource Them

Once you have begun inductive study in earnest, keep files for future use. After completing a study of Ephesians, the result should be a something akin to a file folder well stocked with findings and insights. A separate study on "armor of God" would yield data for the Ephesians file; or, if that folder becomes overstuffed, begin separate ones for various sections of Ephesians. Character studies and word and topical/doctrinal studies, of course, could claim an entire section of such a file cabinet or take up significant space on a computer hard drive.

The goal is to fill your files with studies that contain observations, interpretations of those findings, suitable correlation and application steps. Notes taken during sermons by others can be dropped in these files for use at a future date. Materials can be photocopied and filed as well. The point is this: some of the best articulators of God's Word are assiduous note-takers. They collect their own work as well as the insights of other scholars, preachers, teachers and writers. Such a file cabinet proves especially helpful for correlation and presentation. While praying and meditating on the week's lesson, often something related to that lesson comes to mind. Having a file to consult or contribute to is a tremendous advantage. Furthermore, past inductive work is useful to have on hand if we hit a dry spot in thinking and need some idea generation.

The best "mini-file" that one can have, of course, is the margins and white spaces of the Bible itself. While space for note taking is usually limited: many who engage in inductive study fill the space at the beginning of a particular book with charts and graphs of the book-as-a-whole and major structural laws and recurrences in the book. Color coding of the book (using a different color for each significant word or theme) is another approach, with interpretive questions written in the margin. A quick tip: hard cover Bibles are not durable over the long haul for those who use their Bibles as rigorously as inductive Bible students, so get a leather bound Bible. They last longer. This is important because if you are forced to get a new Bible due to wear and tear, it is frustrating and time-consuming to switch all your notes from one Bible to another. And you will want your notes to run from one decade to the next and not just from one month or year to the next.

Inductive study is work, but accumulation of insight is also somewhat addictive, captivating and energizing. Get a Bible that will last over the long term of your devotional life and educational career.

Teach the Inductive Method while Conveying Content

We would caution against overt reference to "structural laws" or "observation-interpretation-correlation-application" in

Sunday school classes or other settings where your hearers are not used to such terminology. However, many teachers attempt with enviable success direct transference of the inductive study principles in the classroom in abbreviated and simplified form.

Psalm 1 is frequently used when teaching the principles of inductive study because its structural qualities are obvious. When presenting this psalm, after a proper introduction of the method, tell the group that there is a major contrast with accompanying competing characteristics in these paragraphs, and invite them to find it. Have them break down into groups of two or three and get to work. They will easily be able to identify the biblical contrast between the righteous and the wicked. Go to the chalkboard and begin detailing their answers. *What makes the righteous, righteous? And the wicked, wicked?* To fortify the answers of the group the teacher will want to be able to not only draw out the obvious scriptural teachings but also illustrate these with previous insights from the correlation phase of the inductive study.

Another challenge for the smaller group discussion using Psalm 1 could be this: List the verbs in the first verse (walk, stand, sit) and describe the importance of the progression of these verbs (i.e., *walking* in the counsel—thinking; *standing* in the way—doing; *sitting* in the seat—belonging). Once these elements are discovered or explained, ask: *Where are you or your peers tempted to walk in wicked counsel? Or stand in the wrong way of things? Or belong to the wrong group?*

Yet another Psalm 1 query: *With what are the "streams of water" of verse 3 compared (law of comparison)?* The answer seems to be in verse 2—the law of the Lord. *Why is this comparison used this way (interpretation)?*

And, finally, test your group once they have tried their wings a bit and see if they can find the major righteous-wicked effect in the passage. Hint—it's toward the end (v. 6). More interpretation: *What does it mean to have the Lord watching over the righteous; what benefit does this provide? And what does it mean that the wicked will perish? When? How? Why?*

Using the laws of contrast, comparison and causation, and doing a little verb search, it is possible to not only provide a lesson in righteous living but also teach a little inductive Bible study along the way. The discovery method gives the class the opportunity to find information on its own but also affirms its answers. This approach works; we have used it often to great effect with a number of passages.

Use Time-tested Outlines

Scripture Press curriculum has for years used an outline to guide the writers and users of its lesson materials and also to provide a philosophy of corporate Bible study. It is based on three simple words: *Focus—Discover—Respond.*

- *Focus* invites the students to contemplate the lesson just as the teacher has been doing for at least the previous week.

- *Discover* is investigating what Scripture has to say about the subject at hand.

- *Respond* is determining what we are supposed to be doing with the data that has just been presented.

An adaptation of this outline is provided below:

- **Focus** Use an episode, event, occurrence or case study that *illustrates the main point* you will be attempting to make or *raises a question* that you intend to answer. This can come directly from Scripture or can be out of the life-as-a-whole discoveries of the correlation phase of inductive study.

- **Discover** Go to the strategic passage(s) of your inductive

Bible study that help students explore the point you are to make or answer the question you have raised. Here the teacher can pose questions for small group discussion and make points related to the lesson's central thrust.

- **Respond** State the advantage(s) gained if students follow the biblical course of action. Make the advantages believable in their minds by using testimonials, statistics, demonstrations, displays and illustrations.

Lawrence Richards, author and Bible teacher, popularized a similar format in the Hook/Book/Look/Took mnemonic tool. Again, an adaptation:

- **Hook** *Hook* your audience with an exciting, provocative, attention-getting introduction. Tell a story or real-life anecdote, use a demonstration, or offer a case study that grabs attention and helps the class relate to the point(s) you will be trying to make.

- **Book** Get into the *Book*, the Scripture. Use some kind of appropriate transition to move from your hook into the Bible. Relate the biblical data and intersperse illustrative material.

- **Look** Move from the primary use of biblical material to *looking* at the implications of the Scripture at hand. In other words, what does the Bible passage mean for our lives as we saunter out of this classroom?

- **Took** Took is all about response. Here you are encouraging your students to *take* something with them that they can immediately implement. And, as with the "respond" portion of the focus-discover-respond outline, show the benefits through motivational testimonies and illustrations to provide impetus and incentive for students to apply the scriptural principles involved.

Dawson Trotman of *The Navigators* campus organization suggested that the best way to wrap up a talk was HWLW—*His Word the Last Word*. For both *Focus-Discover-Respond* and *Hook/Book/Look/Took* that would be appropriate—bring the strategic passage of Scripture back into the lesson by quoting it exactly as it was found in the Bible. Or, the specific action(s) could be restated and the biblical principle reiterated. Alternately, you might end with an inspirational story.

Since both approaches are similar, let's illustrate the Focus-Discover-Respond model with a passage from Ephesians.

Ephesians 5:22-32: Sample Lesson for Youth/Adults
"Getting Some New Clothes"

Focus

Recount Dad Friedeman, coming home from Friedeman Service Store Saturday evening after a long week's work—dirty, grimy, oil and dirt under fingernails, in a dark mood after working at a job he doesn't really like for money that isn't all that good. But Sunday morning he takes an extended bath, dashes himself with some Old Spice aftershave, puts on his Sunday best and picks up his Bible. His demeanor changes. He is suddenly cheerful, reviewing his Sunday School lesson, ready to go to church to shake hands and laugh with his friends before Sunday school class and worship service. With his fresh duds and different attitude on Sunday, Dad is a new man. This week Dad and his renewed Sunday self (although he was an honest and good man!) got me to thinking a little more carefully about the fifth chapter of Ephesians. Do new clothes and a fresh outlook really make a difference?

Discover

Teacher stands in front of the crowd with six T-shirts on, all apparently dirty, grimy and oily. The first T-shirt hides all the others. Read 5:22-24, about taking off the old self and putting on righteousness and holiness.

Then strip off the first T-shirt to show the next dirty T-shirt with "Falsehood!" written across it in big letters, with magic marker. Read 25a where it says to put off falsehood. . . . (Read only the negative part of all the verses; here tell story about how telling a lie in childhood got you in big trouble!)

Take next T-shirt off to show "Stealing!" (28a) across the chest . . . . (Tell story of how Mom once caught me stealing marshmallows out of the kitchen cabinet. . . .)

Next T-shirt comes off to display "Unwholesome talk!" (29a) . . . . (Tell story of how sister once heard me telling story replete with rather "colorful" language).

Next T-shirt is removed to show "Rage and anger" (31a) . . . . (Tell of how when younger I was perpetually angry but never knew why).

Next T-shirt reveals a clean T-shirt. This T-shirt stays on while reading vs. 25b (Speak truthfully!), 28b (Work!), 29b (Speak to build up others!), 32 (Be kind and compassionate). Illustrate each characteristic (personal illustrations if possible like the negative illustrations above) and add a piece of clothing for each verse (i.e., dress shirt, then cuff links, then tie, then coat).

Respond

"As each of us bows in a word of prayer, place your hands palm down on your knees and visualize yourself surrendering to the Lord one of the following items that Paul suggests we 'put off,' that is problematic in your life:"

"Falsehood?" (Pause for a moment) "Give it to the Lord."

"Stealing?" (Pause) "Give it to the Lord."

"Unwholesome talk?" (Pause) "Give it to the Lord."

> *"Rage and anger?" (Pause) "Give it to the Lord."*
>
> *"Now, friends, place your palms up on your knees and 'put on'/ receive God's goodness:*
>
> *"Truth?" (Pause) "Accept it from the Lord."*
>
> *"Speaking to build up others?" (Pause) "Accept it from the Lord."*
>
> *"Kindness and compassion?" (Pause) "Accept it from the Lord. Amen."*
>
> *"Now, dear friends, we are dressed up and ready to go to worship the Lord. But remember, this is more than a Sunday thing. We are to put on the righteousness and holiness of God twenty-four hours of every day, seven days of every week. If the Lord has talked to you in a special way today about something you really need to 'put off' and something else you need to 'put on' this week call one of your friends who is here today and confess that necessary change of spiritual garment. Tell that friend what kind of progress you are already making this week. Anyone willing to make that 'phone call' commitment? (Leader puts up hand and waits for a show of other hands.) Perhaps we could report back next week. . . ."*

Less Than Full-Blown Approach

Readers of this volume will by now be able to see the efficacy of the inductive Bible study method and be desirous of utilizing the approach in personal devotion, learning enhancement and lesson preparation. Some will recognize that the approach seems to be a lot of work, and six to ten hour study sessions for next Sunday's sixth grade class are hardly what they had in mind. Such readers may be intimidated from using what they recognize as an exciting but incredibly time-consuming approach. In real life, the thinking sometimes goes, *Who has the time?*

The best approach to inductive study is a thorough one, and six to ten hours studying Ephesians-as-a-whole (before breaking it down into its major units) will be necessary if one is to really get a start—yes, just a good start—for a lifetime of learning in the epistle. But, let's say, you've got to give a Sunday school lesson tomorrow and you can spare an hour tonight. Can inductive Bible study help then?

Undoubtedly so. We won't back off the challenge to the readers that the more time spent, the greater accrued benefit in the classroom. But we will also confess that we have asked *Who, What, When, Where, How* and *Why* an hour before presenting a lesson, or searched for *structural laws* in a unit and asked what the laws meant in light of the author's worldview in the waning moments before a small group Bible study. Or we have tried to think of something out of our life history (*correlation*) to punch up that point we were going to make in verse 4 as our names were being introduced moments before a speaking engagement. A few times we have wondered how the audience can use all this great insight—actually *apply* it in their lives—knowing that if we present this Bible study to our teenagers this morning with no challenge they most certainly will deem us as irrelevant as, in that moment, we are.

Like many things in life, inductive Bible study can be done with high proficiency poring over the holy data for hours, days or weeks at a time. But it is not only for those precious times of concentrated leisure. The principles of inductive Bible study will also reward moments of deadline-driven desperation with insights that seem to leap off the page at just the right moment.

CHAPTER 12

Inductive Bible Study: A Quick Summary

The late author A.W. Tozer once defined the word "enemy" as whatever kept him from his Bible and from meditating on things external. This is simply another way of saying that the Scriptures had become his truest friend.

While most Christians understand Tozer's perspective, all too few feel it with the same degree of passion. For many Christian educators what keeps us from our Bible is nothing more than simple ignorance of how to plumb its depths for dynamic insights. This volume has been an attempt to challenge this unnecessary blockage to the growth and joy that comes through understanding God's word, and to enhance its power as a means of grace in our lives.

GOD'S REVELATION IS REVEALED THROUGH INDUCTIVE METHOD

Inductive Bible study is a methodical process by which an inductive approach is employed to investigate God's revelation to humankind. With the inductive method, Scripture is engaged with a clean mental slate, and intensive investigative methods are used, step-by-step, to honestly try to arrive at the truth God intends to communicate. This discipline is intensely valuable to anyone whose task it is to distill truth, relay it to others and teach them how to find it themselves.

INDUCTIVE BIBLE STUDY IS A TWENTIETH CENTURY RENAISSANCE

The growing popularity of induction as a distinct Bible study method is a rather modern phenomenon, its development being traced to the mid-1900's. Although Bible study in various forms has been around as long as the biblical canon, Dr. Wilbert W. White, founder of *The Biblical Seminary* in New York, probably deserves the title "father of inductive Bible study." Distinguished students carried into subsequent decades his torch for independent, competent and original study of the Bible in the vernacular of the learning community. Most prominent of these is Dr. Robert Traina, author of *Methodical Bible Study*, who had a long and distinguished career as a professor at Asbury Theological Seminary.

INDUCTIVE METHODOLOGY BEGINS WITH OBSERVATION

Observation, the act and the art of seeing things as they really are, is the first step of inductive methodology. Because a proper building of this foundational step is so crucial, care must be taken to ensure a thorough and scientific approach.

- Ask the obvious questions: *Who, What, When, Where, How* and *Why?*

- Look for key words or phrases.

- Pay attention to purpose, literary form, comparisons, contrasts, questions, connectives, grammar and tone.

- Look for commands, promises and positive or negative characteristics of individuals or situations.

- Make a chart to graphically summarize your findings.

- Employ all these means to see what upon first glance might remain hidden.

THE STRUCTURAL LAWS FACILITATE OBSERVATION

Utilization of the structural laws assists us in understanding how materials are arranged within books and scriptural passages. Searching for these laws, which the biblical author uses to unify or organize his message, is a primary mode by which the student will observe hidden insights. Upon taking a step back and getting the "bird's eye view," the reader can detect the means by which a book, then a passage, hangs together: repetition, preparation/introduction, comparison, contrast, climax, cruciality/pivot, interchange, particularization/generalization, cause and effect, interrogation and summarization. Interrelationships between the laws can be significant.

INTERPRETATION FOLLOWS OBSERVATION AS THE SECOND MAJOR STEP

Interpretation follows close behind observation and involves determining the meaning and significance of a unit of study and its parts. The process of interpretation comprises asking probing questions and drawing responsible conclusions. Again, the questions *Who, What, When, Where, How* and *Why* are imposed, but this time in a much more detailed manner and coupled with the particular structural laws detected in a passage. From these, the most significant questions are selected and the "answering" process begins, staying mindful of context, genre, or literary style and figures of speech.

CORRELATION CONNECTS TRUTH THROUGHOUT BIBLICAL PASSAGES

Correlation completes the inductive process by examining relevant data from other biblical passages, from history and from life, and linking them together into a holistic Biblical approach. Correlation is an attitude as well as a step in procedure as the creative, insightful mind relates biblical truth to other biblical truth, to contemporary media, to church history, to local and even world history and so forth.

APPLICATION MOVES FROM THE TEXT TO THE WORLD

Once we find out what God thinks and how He operates, through the process of observation, interpretation and correlation, the next logical step is to live it out. This is application. The acquisition of biblical truth is relatively meaningless if it doesn't make a difference at a practical level. The Bible student must determine which truths are practical in the contemporary situation and then use devotional means to apply these findings to his own heart, the inward application. Then he must ask penetrating questions in order to apply these same Biblical truths to his everyday life, the outward application.

SHIFT INDUCTIVE STUDY INTO THE PERSONAL MODE

Character studies are effective because people relate best to people. So focusing on one of the more than 3,000 names in the Bible makes for fascinating and endless fuel for focused studies. In undertaking a concentrated study such as this, the making of a life line or time line is quite helpful. Also, special attention should be given to the character's name, the birth, family background, early life and training, conversion, historical setting, geography, spiritual life, major accomplishments and death. Again, structural laws can be useful in the observation process and reference works are helpful in understanding the culture within which an individual lived. Devotional application can be significant as one ponders qualities to emulate and characteristics to avoid.

INDUCTIVE STUDIES WITH TOPICAL AND WORD STUDIES

Topical studies address a felt need and word studies are helpful in facilitating the investigation of a topic. Many vehicles can be "topic-starters": the imagination, radio, TV, news, sports and life situations such as tragedies, politics, illnesses, personal struggles, friendships, work opportunities and so forth. A concordance can pinpoint specific words which merit studies in themselves as well as lead to the identification of related topics. Also useful are chain reference Bibles and topical Bibles. Again, the observation-interpretation-correlation-application process is employed to uncover insights which can be spiritually digested and effectively communicated.

Finis

Why, in the final analysis, are we such advocates of inductive study of the Holy Scripture? It's an old story but bears repeating: A man, walking to his job every day, stopped to synchronize his watch with the grandfather clock showcased in the clockmaker's store. The clockmaker became fascinated with the man's ritualistic regularity and so struck up a conversation with him one day. The clockmaker asked the man what he did for a living. The man said that he worked at the factory a few blocks away and since it was his responsibility to ring the closing bell every day at 5:00 p.m. he synchronized his watch—that admittedly didn't work very well—with the clockmaker's grandfather clock. The clockmaker suddenly became a bit red-faced and obviously embarrassed and, when asked about his sudden uneasiness, he admitted that his grandfather clock didn't work all that well either, which is why he adjusted it to the factory bell every day at 5:00 p.m.

Without the Bible earnestly studied and diligently applied, we only swap less-than-satisfactory answers in the pursuit of meaning and of truth. Inductive Bible study is the best way to arrive at the answers we all desire. When we adjust our life to the Word of God after appropriate prayer, observation, interpretation, correlation and application, we will know that our lives are tuned to something reliable.

Devout Jews have always been known as "the people of the Book." This may be a noble moniker, but Christians will perhaps choose to be known as "people of the Persons"—Father, Son and Holy Spirit. Still, our forebears in the faith have a point: it is the Book that informs our knowledge, our experience, our encounter with those Persons and with the world to whom this triune God calls us.

The material expressed in this volume has changed our lives. Our hope and prayer is that you will, through the means of grace called inductive study, let it change yours, too.